# Spiritual Development

Jörgen Smit

# Spiritual Development

## Meditation in daily life

Floris Books

Translated by Donald Maclean


First published in German under the title
*Geisteschulung und Lebenspraxis.*
*Die Grundstein–Meditation als Zukunftsimpuls*
by Verlag am Goetheanum, Dornach, 1987.

First published in English by Floris Books in 1991.

British Library CIP available

ISBN 0-86315-096-9

Printed in Great Britain
by Dotesios Ltd, Trowbridge, Wilts.

# Contents

Foreword                                    7

Lecture 1                                   9

Lecture 2                                  27

Lecture 3                                  42

Lecture 4                                  57

Lecture 5                                  74


Notes                                      89

The Foundation Stone verse                 90

# Foreword

These lectures were given by Jörgen Smit to an international conference of some two hundred young people held in The Hague at Christmas 1986. The participants at this conference all had a basic knowledge of anthroposophy and the content of the lectures assumes this.

This gathering arose out of a wish to come to a deeper understanding of the fundamentals of anthroposophy and of the "Foundation Stone" of the Anthroposophical Society. In 1923, a year after the tragedy of the burning of the original Goetheanum building, the centre of the Anthroposophical Society in Dornach, Switzerland, Rudolf Steiner re-founded the Anthroposophical Society at a week-long conference starting on December 24. On this occasion, known as the Christmas Conference or the Christmas Foundation, Rudolf Steiner laid a "foundation stone" not in the form of a stone (as had been the case in 1913 with the first Goetheanum building), but in the form of a mantric verse which would be a "foundation" in the hearts of all members of the newly founded General Anthroposophical Society.

The full text of the Foundation Stone verse appears on page 90.

# 1

The Christmas Conference of 1923 is a special event in the history of the Anthroposophical Movement and Society. One year previously the first Goetheanum had been destroyed by arson. The first Goetheanum was the artistic expression of the living element of anthroposophy. It was an all–embracing work of art in which all the different arts could work together. Architecture, sculpture, modelling, painting, music, recitation, drama and eurythmy all came to expression there. But anthroposophy lived not only in this external expression but also, and more importantly, in the souls of those who were gathered together in the Goetheanum. The two aspects together formed a unity. The works of art and the Goetheanum itself were not separated or isolated from the inner life of those people who were gathered there. Then came the fire destroying the physical manifestation of this great artistic activity. A heap of ashes lay upon the Dornach Hill. Only the bare workshop remained, and the sculpture, the *Representative of Mankind.* A heap of ashes was all that was left. In one night, ten years' artistic work had vanished.

What was the situation in the human community, now bereft of its base in which all this was to have lived? Was it a close–knit community in which all that could live strongly? No, in the spring of 1923 the Anthroposophical Society was itself a heap of ruins, split and fragmented into several groups openly warring with each other, crippled and incapable of meeting attacks from without, immature with regard to the great demands of humanity. The movement for the threefold social order had been abandoned two years previously: success in this was no longer possible, partly through the incompetence of the Society, partly due to other causes. Because of inflation, various anthroposophical undertakings were in a very difficult situation and on the verge of bankruptcy or indeed bankrupt. That was the situation of the Anthroposophical Society in the spring of 1923, so that Rudolf Steiner himself had to say that the Goetheanum lay in ruins on the hill, and the Anthroposophical Society was itself a heap of ruins.[1]

What could be done in such a situation? Rudolf Steiner considered the options very realistically and precisely. He considered the possibility of abandoning all the great tasks, not indefinitely but temporarily, as they could not be carried out just then, and withdrawing to work with a very small group of people, in a strictly-run esoteric school.

At that time there were 12 000 members in the Anthroposophical Society; today there are 43 000. Rudolf Steiner would not have taken the 12 000 into this work, for they were a heap of ruins as far as working together was concerned. He would have called together twelve or twenty-four and would have worked intensively with them in a very small circle, for the future. But he did not act in this way, though he really did consider this option and weighed it carefully. Then he did the very opposite. He took a mighty step forward, much more strongly than before. He gathered all his strength for a mighty impulse for the future, dedicating himself to humanity by a further step in the realization of anthroposophy so that the new esoteric school, the Free Academy for Spiritual Science as a Mystery

School, should be at the same time the kernel of a completely open society: the kernel of the General Anthroposophical Society as a world society.

That was the impulse of the Christmas Conference. It was a tremendous step forward with a much stronger realization of anthroposophy than before, taken in such a dark and sombre situation. It should not be underestimated how difficult that time was.

That situation, seen in the context of world history, has its counterpart on a minor scale in what every modern person faces today, for what modern person has not at some time had a dark and sombre period when everything he has tried to accomplish has failed, and the external opposition has been too great? Then taking stock he has had to admit that his purposes have been utterly defeated. He faces utter darkness, and he may say to himself: "What now? I cannot go on in this way. I shall have to do something quite different. I shall have to content myself with more mundane matters and renounce the grand aims which I had set myself." Or what is worse, he may contemplate suicide. On the other hand, in such a situation a person today can do something new, something creative, just when the situation is at its most difficult. He can rise above himself and develop a greater and stronger will, of course on a smaller scale than what happened at the Christmas Conference. But the comparison is not wrong, for what was achieved by Rudolf Steiner on a large scale with significance for world history can be achieved by any one of us on a smaller scale. This is achieved through the *werdende Mensch*. This *werdende Mensch* is the inner spirit–man that is growing, is becoming, is developing within us. The *werdende Mensch* never gives up, has the perseverance to go on through the darkness and the strength to take a fresh step forward. The strength to rise above oneself, even by a little, is the power of the *werdende Mensch,* the power of the spirit–being of man. It does not happen by nature, it does not happen by instinct. Everything natural and instinctive would founder before the challenge. The new and creative force surges up in the individual and he rises above himself.

If we look at the whole situation of mankind at present, in the year 1986, we can say that mankind as a whole needs this new and creative force. If we look at the series of catastrophes of this year (Chernobyl for example) we see a great picture that speaks: "Now is the time to wake up! We cannot go on this way any further. If we go on as before, we shall end up in the abyss. Something new must be done. There must be no thought of flight or of despair, but rather something new, creative, that leads out of this sombre situation. That is the Christmas Conference. It is the *werdende Mensch* in the whole of mankind, and this new impulse is completely open to the world, no sect, no narrow, limited, dogmatic group, but a society open to the world with an esoteric schooling as its kernel. And what is the kernel of the esoteric schooling? It is the human being who rises above himself to new planes of knowledge. If we simply remain stagnant in what has been we only reflect the past. A true cognition is creative and marches forward to new possibilities. Here the spirit activity of the individual works within the whole of mankind, it is not shut away inside the individual. This activity, this cognition, is contained in and gives form to the "Foundation Stone" verses.[2]

What do we observe, what do we perceive in the Foundation Stone Meditation? It is the human soul. The single individual soul is addressed, or we might equally say the single individual soul addresses itself: "Man, know thyself." Those ancient mystery words which have gone through the millennia rang out in the last Michael Ages to the Greek soul, but in quite a different way. The divine–spiritual in the human being was intrinsically so strong that the individual had only to reflect upon it in order to discover his spiritual origin. Therefore at that time there was a certain cultural unity feature, a spiritual inheritance, we might also say. It was enough to enable the individual to act out of it. It still shone into the soul, and the soul was borne along by it. Today that is not sufficient. If today the human being contemplates such a unity of spiritual inheritance, he can easily be led astray in a one–sided illusionary manner that is not truly human. The great difference today is that the human being no longer has within him this great inner inheritance of the sustaining spirit, but has been abandoned by it. Now it is the individual action which predominates. The evil powers of the adversaries, Lucifer and Ahriman, come to the fore. If the individual were only to contemplate the uniform divinity in himself, as in the former age of Michael, then a Luciferic–spiritual or an Ahrimanic–spiritual would appear. Present–day man must direct these words, "Man, know thyself" in three directions, otherwise it will not be true. Truth speaks in a threefold way. The human being seeks himself in three directions, even though the evil powers are working with him to left and right. Only in this threefold questing can the present–day individual work his way forward in self–cognition. Thus we hear three times: "Soul of man! Thou livest in the limbs ... in the pulsing of the heart and lungs ... in the resting head." Three quite different directions! In the eurythmy presentation of the meditation, darkness comes between each of these. So it is not something uniform in which we seek the spiritual in general, but it is separated into three distinct directions, so that each direction can work in its own particular way — all three with the challenge to increased activity: "Practise, practise, practise." If this "practise" is left out and we seek self–cognition so that it is just a verification of what has been and of what is still there — a penetrating analysis of what is there — that is not the Christmas Conference. That would be psychoanalysis or something else. Then you simply remain stuck in what has been and observe more and more closely what is there. But that is not what we seek. We must go forward. If the soul is to seek the truth she must be doing something. If she just sits there inertly and just wants to get truth she will get Lucifer and Ahriman — one illusion after another. What, however, present–day man needs is increased inner activity whereby he grows slowly out beyond himself, otherwise his existence is threatened, that is, his own individual existence and the existence of all mankind.

Let us now consider more closely the first direction: "Soul of man! Thou livest in the limbs." Now the challenge comes from the inmost part: "Practise spirit–memory."* What does that mean? Let us disregard "spirit" and concentrate upon "memory" in order to see clearly what is meant when "spirit" and "memory" are connected. We should then have an exercise to strengthen memory. Everyone has some kind of memory; it can be good, bad or indifferent. Memory can be strengthened by practice. Then it would be "practise remembering, so that you can better retain in your mind everything you did yesterday, the day before yesterday and ten years ago, indeed what you have done all your life." That would be ordinary remembering — not "spirit–

---

* *Übe Geist–Erinnern* is variously translated as *spirit–recalling* (Michael Wilson, Arvia Mackaye), *spirit–recollection* (George Adams) and *spirit–remembering* (Richard Seddon). See *The Foundation Stone,* Rudolf Steiner Press, London, 1979.

memory." That would simply be remembering on the surface, but now we are concerned with "spirit–memory" in the depths of the soul.

In the introductory chapter of Rudolf Steiner's *Knowledge of the Higher Worlds* there is an exercise in which the disciple of the spirit is told to set aside short periods in which he looks back on his past life — but not just using his memory to recall exactly what has happened — but rather from a higher standpoint, as if he were someone else, trying to distinguish the essential from the non–essential (that is, that which has *essence* or *being* from that which has *no essence* or *no being*). If I try to distinguish the essential from the non–essential then I penetrate the surface to reach into the depths. What really is the past? What came out of it? What was the essence or being *(das Wesen)* of the happening? What was my own essence or being in this happening?

Here we enter the field of will, for in memory we look back on the *actions* of our lives, what we have done with our limbs in the world, what we have done with other people and with nature.

Here we have first a surface layer where we try to achieve certain aims, be they near or distant: "Now I'm going here, now there: I'm going to get up and get dressed and then off to the greater aims of my profession." All activities of will directed to particular ends. All very important. They constitute the whole field of activity within this surface layer. But however great and true these particular aims may be there is still a deeper will: that is the will of the *werdende Mensch* and this will goes out beyond all the particular aims of our ordinary will, for it is the deeper will in each individual. Even when he is a small child, the individual has this will at work in him from one day to the next, from one year to the next, from one decade to the next, at work right through all the crises of life. It is the will of the *werdende Mensch* lifting the individual out beyond himself. These deeper forces are of significance for the whole of life and reveal themselves in such exercises of retrospection in which we look back on life from a higher standpoint: the striving eternal individual at work in matter, seeking his own being and origin. That is the meaning of "spirit–memory."

When the practice of spirit–memory becomes strong and the forces of the *werdende Mensch* emerge strongly we begin to discover something new in other people and in the world around us. This new thing is indeed also the *werdende Mensch,* for the *werdende Mensch* is not isolated within each individual. As I discover it in myself, I discover it in other people, in those people with whom I am joined in the workings of destiny.

How then does this destiny work from one earth–life to another, from one cultural epoch to another? One important feature of our destiny is that the consequences of our actions stream out into the world. The inner spiritual being of every individual lives not only in the acts which he performs but also in the consequences of his acts. The individual's spiritual being lives and works on in those people who have been affected by his actions. In this way all our higher beings are united. They live in each other. From this interweaving of our higher beings the pattern of the individual's destiny is woven. The consequences of the individual's deeds in one life return to him as his fate in a future earth life. If we take no account of this law and reject our destiny, we really show hatred to our true selves, to our true being. This true being weaves our destiny for us out of love, that out of love we may grow, and out of love search again for our true being. Then we can be united with the world, with the true being of others and even with the heaviest blows of fate, for this love embraces not only happiness but pain and sorrow on the path towards reunion with our true being, with the world totality.

In this first exercise of "spirit–memory" we see a descent into the depths of soul to that original Being from whom we come and in whom we first can truly live. "And thou wilt truly *live.*" The opposite also obtains: if we do not do this, we do not truly live. Of course it is a constant search, not a sudden transition from truly living to not truly living, it is a seeking in the direction: "Practise *spirit–memory* ... and thou wilt truly *live* in the World–Being of Man." Substance of love — that is the first direction.

In the eurythmy presentation of the Foundation Stone Meditation it now turns dark: then comes the second, quite different direction. All our attention is now focused on what arises new at every moment and comes into being in the "Pulsing of the heart and lungs": on all that is becoming, the Deeds of World–Becoming; all that is new that takes place in feeling, in relation to the world around. That is a *meeting.* In our contact with our surroundings, with the people whom we meet, something new can come into being. Then we face the question: "Wilt thou unite thyself with something that is greater than thyself?" Two possible courses of action immediately present themselves to us. One course of action is to unite in such a way that we surrender our own identity and independence: we become utterly absorbed into our surroundings — this is hysteria. The other course of action is to assert ourselves, to assert our identity. In that case no union takes place. Both courses are wrong, for the mantra says: "Thine own I unite with the World–I." And this again has to do with the direction of the exercise.

17

Here we do not have to recall the spirit being within us, but ask: "What is happening at this moment?" Contemplate what is happening. But there can be a contemplation which is not a *spirit*–contemplation. Then one only directs one's attention to the surface. Now all our attention must become more deeply conscious. When we practise concentration and contemplation we must become conscious of the spirituality arising from within us and uniting itself with what is coming from other people and from the whole world surrounding us. This uniting takes place in feeling. But the essential quality of feeling required for this meeting can be lost in two ways: through coldness if we shut ourselves off from the world, through warmth if we stream out into the world and lose ourselves. But in the true unification with the world, the world begins to speak in feeling, it has the power of speech. Man speaks with the world, the world speaks with man. Here we see a direction quite different from that in the first mantra. In the second we practise concentrating on what is happening in the heart–feeling at each moment in the intercourse with the world and with other people. "Practise *spirit–contemplation* and thou wilt truly feel," that means too that when you do not feel in this way you are not truly feeling, but you are cold or over–enthusiastic, gushing.* "Practise *spirit–contemplation* and thou wilt truly feel." Then in the eurythmy presentation it grows dark again. Now comes the third and again quite different direction: "Practise *spirit–observation*."†

---

\* *Geist–Besinnen* has been variously translated into English. The standard translation has *spirit–awareness.* George Adams has *spirit–meditation,* and Arvia MacKaye *spirit–communing.*

† *Geist–Erschauen.* Michael Wilson, Arvia Mackaye and Richard Seddon all use *spirit–beholding.* George Adams has *spirit–penetration.*

Now we are concerned with the objectiveness of the world–totality, not with our personal opinion; we are concerned with the world–thoughts to which we have to find access. But first there must be a basis, and this is what is most dead in the human being, the most shut–off in itself, the head. The *head* is an end in the divine creative activity, and this termination can be a basis because we can *rest* in it. "Soul of man! Thou livest in the resting head." Only on this basis is it possible to seek access to the world–thoughts. For these do not come immediately. What comes immediately is again superficial, ideas and opinions, not the world–thoughts but superficial picture–images from without. To attain to the world–thoughts we have to strive and search for truth. A door has to be opened up; a key has to be created. This is done by activity: "Practise spirit–observation." The world–thoughts are to be made to appear in the mind, in such a way that the real sense and meaning of the whole world, the world aims, the divine aims become conscious to us in the world–thoughts. A new door is opened for the will, a different door from that of the first exercise.

In the radiance of the world–thoughts the human being can become free in his will. Before the individual awakes to this radiance he acts according to his instincts, and his actions are determined by outer and inner circumstances. Only after this awakening does this gift of light in free thought lead also to free will, and only then does thinking take up its true place in the whole of world evolution. "And thou wilt truly *think*." Up till then to a certain extent our thinking was not true.

Here we have a way, a searching, a direction of striving. In all three directions we begin with a starting point given by nature to which we then add something new. The soul is creatively engaged in this process of becoming in the whole of mankind. We see what now must really come to pass, how it is bursting forth, for it is a challenge of life, a challenge to the existence of all humanity.

On the one hand this striving has what is most intimate and inward in the individual. In him this new spiritual growth is realized in the three directions we have mentioned. On the other hand and at the same time there is complete openness to the world.

When we now look at the Christmas Conference we can see that the two opposites, the inmost intimate and the openness to the world are both invoked in paragraph 4 of the Statutes of the Anthroposophical Society:

"The Anthroposophical Society is in no sense a secret society, but is entirely public. Anyone can become a member without regard to nationality, social standing, religion, scientific or artistic conviction, who considers as justified the existence of an institution such as the Goetheanum in Dornach, in its capacity as a School of Spiritual Science."

Here we see that every person is welcome to become a member of the General Anthroposophical Society regardless of his scientific, artistic or religious viewpoint. A member can have any scientific cast of thought when he enters the General Anthroposophical Society, he does not have to surrender it at the door. He can have any religious conviction, whether Christian, Muslim, Buddhist, Hindu or atheist, all are welcome. His attitude and conviction do not have to be given up, for he can join regardless. The Society is really open to all mankind, that is the starting point. We come from quite different backgrounds: one comes from a strong Protestant home, another from a deeply Roman Catholic background, while another is of a Marxist–atheistic conviction which colours his whole thinking, and another comes from a Buddhist direction. In the Anthroposophical Society we have members who have not only *been* Buddhist priests but still *are* and yet are members. Also in the Anthroposophical Society there are Muslims, Hindus and Orthodox Jews who reject Christianity. Thus it is possible for people coming from all parts of the world to awaken to a direction of striving which goes out beyond their background. It then depends upon the individual how much he is transformed. This is the great task of the *werdende Mensch.* What becomes of my inherited nature? I may join and take part in this process of the *werdende Mensch,* but each individual must work at what he has inherited. Everything which comes from the past, whether it be from Hinduism, Christianity, Judaism or Buddhism, cannot maintain its form in the face of the *werdende Mensch.*

The individual is thus called upon to work out of the inner force of the *werdende Mensch* in order to discover new things within himself and to transform himself. Thus we see that anthroposophy is completely undogmatic. What is important is that something really spiritual happens beyond what the individual had hitherto done, thought and felt. Then the *werdende Mensch* comes more to the fore. Thus all activity in the Anthroposophical Society really is of an experimental nature. What do I mean by that? If you just sit down and think something out, that is not experimental. In an experiment you discover something new. An experiment can be external–physical. But we are not concerned with that. Here we are concerned with an experimental approach to the spiritual: to discover something new in every moment. In the Anthroposophical Movement it is never an aim to repeat certain thought–forms and to say: those are the correct thought–forms: I know them off by heart. That is not anthroposophy. All thoughts are important in anthroposophy, but they have to be worked out exactly.

They are anthroposophical only in so far as they are *transparent*. A thought which is not transparent is just a formula that something is such and such: it is a dogma. Transparent thoughts are avenues to spiritual facts. What are spiritual facts? They are meetings with the spiritual worlds, with spiritual beings. Only in this there are many degrees. We meet spiritual facts in anthroposophy, otherwise it is not alive. But the first encounter with such facts is of the nature of a spiritual sense of touch. Imagine that someone is standing in a physical space: he is blind, deaf, has no taste, no sense of smell, he has only a sense of touch; a hypo-thetical picture. When he begins to move about in space he will soon come upon and feel a physical object. Moving in the spirit–world we also begin with a sense of touch. We work in a spiritual field, but now we do not just think thoughts, but in the thought we encounter a spiritual reality which we feel. Not yet do we see anything, hear anything spiritual. We only feel something. That is the first stage. After this first dark spiritual sense of touch it becomes lighter and lighter, but even with the first sense of touch there is something new.

During the year 1923 the Anthroposophical Societies of various countries were formed: Norway, Holland, Switzer-land and so on. Among these the Anthroposophical Society of Great Britain was founded on September 2, 1923 in London. Two weeks before that, on August 19, Rudolf Steiner was in Penmaenmawr. I shall now quote two sentences from what he said there:

"And this difference of the anthroposophical movement from other movements we should endeavour to make clear to the world: its comprehensiveness, its lack of bias and prejudice, its freedom from dogma; the fact that it is only an experimental method of what is human in general and of the general phenomena of the world."[3]

This was said in Great Britain, the nation of experimenters and scientific researchers. This requirement of anthroposophy to be an experimental method, Rudolf Steiner made particularly clear in England. But it is meant as *spiritual* experimenting: the whole of anthroposophy as a spiritual experimental method without set dogmas, indeed the thought–aggregate of anthroposophy is not to be taken as postulates of a faith or belief. Therefore Rudolf Steiner said that it was desirable that anthroposophy might have "a different name every week." Just imagine the confusion if anthroposophy were to have its name changed every week. Then we should be on an unstable ship in a stormy sea. That would be too much. We have to have a bit of stability: anthroposophy will still be anthroposophy next week. But we should know that Rudolf Steiner actually wished to find a different name every week, so that we are not tempted to think that we have got hold of the essence once and for all. That would not be anthroposophy. Anthroposophy is an experimental method, an experimental approach in which something new takes place creatively in three directions.

Thus we see that on the one hand the General Anthroposophical Society has the intent of being completely open to the world, but on the other within it there must take place the deepest most intimate *spirit–memory, spirit–contemplation, spirit–observation,* that is to say unmitigated spirit-experience, directly on the road to initiation into cognition of the higher worlds.

Along with paragraph 4, the following sentence is found in a letter of July 13, 1924 to the members:

"In this way, through the work of the would–be active members, the Anthroposophical Society may become a true preparatory school for the school of Initiates."[4]

Just consider the whole implication: everything that takes place in the Anthroposophical Society should be a preparatory school for the school of initiation! That means: experience of the spirit, direct personal experience of the spirit! And at the same time it says in paragraph 4 that no one will be refused admission, but everything which is brought into the General Anthroposophical Society will be regarded as a valid starting–point. But something has to happen from there, and so there is a condition: that the person "considers as justified the existence of an institution such as the Goetheanum in Dornach, in its capacity as a school of Spiritual Science." That is the way to knowledge of the higher worlds. The member is woken to the fact that cognition of the higher worlds can be developed. If you reject that, then you must seek elsewhere. It is a question of the *werdende Mensch* at the turning point of cognition. Then we begin to work with what is given. In this great crucible of the past we go forward to prepare the seeds for the future.

Now this decisive founding of the Anthroposophical Society did not take place at a peaceful time. Imagine hypothetically a calm and peaceful time when people could meet and begin to work at something which could grow undisturbed. That was not the case. It was the twentieth century and it was no peaceful time but rather the most violent storm in the history of mankind was raging — the greatest turbulence, the greatest deployment of the adversarious powers to extirpate everything that anthroposophy cherished. The Christmas Conference, this seed of future development, was not set in a peaceful time but in a stormy warring time when all strength had to be mustered in order to carry on with this impulse. This storm, this war did not stop in front of the doors of the Anthroposophical Society because in the souls of the anthroposophists there was storm and war.

When we look back on the years which have passed since the Christmas Conference, these sixty–three years, we see much that is beautiful and positive. All that has happened in the thousands of human souls, where something new has been possible in each life through anthroposophy, a new comprehension of destiny, immeasurable seeds of the future live in each individual and take external effect in the schools, curative homes, eurythmy, agriculture and so on. If however we take it all together we must admit that it is all too little in comparison with the needs of the present. We must acknowledge realistically that it has fallen short. No excuse, no use ascribing causes, for we are right in the midst of this storm and this warring time externally and internally, and we can see that only a little has succeeded. In one thing in particular we have fallen short by a long way: immediately before the Christmas Conference Rudolf Steiner held some lectures on the Anthroposophical Movement and Society.[5] On June 11, 1923 he said that a particular task of the Anthroposophical Society was to attain to a common–I. That is no abstract thought, for he meant that there is a being, a corporate I, in the whole Anthroposophical Society, a spiritual being who is active in all of us. This task, he added, is very difficult. Generally it is not difficult to attain to a community–I in a group of people. But in that case it is at the cost of truth, as for example in some party or sect where really a spiritual being holds that group of people together but with loss of truth. In the present–day a community–I can only become a true one when it comes about through each individual — uncompromising search for truth by each individual, and nevertheless one can attain to the next stage of the common–I in mutual discussion. Then Rudolf Steiner said that in this respect the Anthroposophical Society in 1923 — just before the Christmas Conference — was not even at the beginning. He did not say that something had already started but that it was "not even at the beginning." The society lies completely in the future. This is what we must work at in the next days. This tremendous distance between the individual and a community which is not a sect but which is to create a community—I. How will that be possible?

# 2

Yesterday I tried to show the whole span of our work in the Anthroposophical Society from two opposite viewpoints. One viewpoint was the *openness to the world* as expressed in paragraph 4 of the Statutes of the Anthroposophical Society. There a person is welcome as a member irrespective of his scientific, artistic or religious convictions, irrespective too of his own personal opinions. There is no dogma, no thought content to which he must subscribe in order to become a member. It must also be possible for any sort of person to come into the Anthroposophical Society and feel at home in it. What does this mean, that a person can feel at home? Simply that there is an innermost longing, regardless of where we have come from, to attain to a deeper knowledge. This is the common factor: we do not want to stop where we are, we want to go deeper.

Then came the other viewpoint which was to regard the Anthroposophical Society — to use Rudolf Steiner's expression — as a real preparation for the *school of initiation,* so that life in the Anthroposophical Society is so intense that there is a spiritual experience in every meeting, in every assembly. It is not just a matter of absorbing certain thoughts and retaining them in one's memory, but of thinking actively and thereby perceiving spiritual facts; and that is always new, deep and surprising. When we regard this, and then look round in the various branches, in study groups, we see how difficult this is. You have to work out something thoroughly in thought. Then you slowly come to direct spiritual experience. That is why continuity is necessary.

It is difficult when new participants appear on the scene of such intensive work. When a group of ten, twenty or thirty people has been working together at something for months and is beginning to become spiritually intense, and suddenly a new person enters, they have to start all over again. The newcomer, quite justifiably, asks basic questions about this and that. You feel that the questions are sincere, for you have also asked these questions, but in the mean-time you have progressed a bit further, and now you have to begin all over again. For this reason there gradually arose in some groups a desire to become somewhat exclusive. In these branches it is almost impossible for others to gain entry, and when a newcomer does come everybody turns round to see who it is. Now you must imagine how the newcomer feels when he comes in and everybody has a good look at him. That is an awkward situation and the newcomer is inclined to disappear again immediately.

Then there are other groups who do the very opposite. They feel it their great task to be open to the world; they are open to everyone. You can go straight in off the street, as it were, without even asking; and every time they meet there are new people there. Therefore each time you have to start again right at the beginning without any reser-vations. Then you have the questions: What is this all about? Is there a spiritual world at all? That has to be tested. What is reincarnation really? Is it true, or is it perhaps only an illusion? Every time you have to start afresh, as if you knew nothing. That is very stimulating and challenging but it is very extreme, just as if an anthroposophical meeting was being held in the market square. All the questions of the day come streaming in with the new people. Then in those groups some members always announce: "We can't go on like this! We must work at anthroposophy. What we are doing is not anthroposophy." Then the others say: "Oh yes it is, we are working in public and it flows out into the whole of humanity." And the first again: "Have we studied the hierarchies in the last three years? Not a bit. That would have been too difficult, we have to prepare it slowly and build a basis in order to come to an understanding of the various spiritual beings, and we can't do that so quickly." And so it is abandoned, and the group begins again with Goethe's *Metamorphosis of the Plant.* It is justified, but it is one extreme of a great spectrum.

Very often a branch or a study group develops one-sidedly towards one or other of these extremes. It is difficult to lead a group in such as way that the whole range is catered for. But there are several days in the week, so that it is possible to arrange different groupings and different ways of working so that all stages can be accommodated. Organization of the work! But here we come to a deep riddle and to difficult tasks and therefore it is important to study this problem in more detail.

For this we must make a short historical survey in order to get to the critical point. What was the relationship between the path of initiation and exoteric culture in the sixteenth, seventeenth, eighteenth and nineteenth centuries? In those centuries there was initiation in the Rosicrucian communities, but only for the few, behind closed doors. When the Rosicrucians went out into the world they achieved much that was fruitful. They did not hide themselves away or work selfishly for themselves, but they made no attempt to make the path of initiation come alive in cultural activities, in art, science or other fields. However the mainstream of materialistic civilization with its science was developing in the direction of technology, and that was very good and necessary in the history of the world. People in Europe and America were directing their attention to matter in experiments and in those intellectual concepts which found a solid base in the material–physical.

At the beginning of the twentieth century the situation was absolutely new. The path that civilization was taking was leading to the abyss. Formerly this path did not lead into the abyss, but it now does. Of course the development of science and technology cannot stop, but it cannot remain the only activity because it is no longer sufficient for the needs of mankind. It is a one–sided development leading to the destruction of nature. Souls, too, are being destroyed. In the twentieth century mankind is hovering on the brink of destruction and needs to wake to a consciousness of the spiritual. Indeed in the twentieth century one cannot live a life of true human dignity unless one wakes to the being of the spirit which is the source of the capacity to reshape one's life. What does that entail? That means that from the twentieth century onwards, initiation cannot remain outside everyday life as a source of inspiration for only a few people, but must be set right in the middle of the life of our civilization so that it can work there to transform our lives.

Anthroposophy is not only a personal matter (of course it is a personal, individual matter when it concerns the enrichment of one's own soul life) but a task for mankind dictated by the necessity of history. There are stages in every individual's life, as one quickly discovers, but how long does one stay at the first stage where anthroposophy is felt as indispensable for one's own soul? How long does it take before one passes from this solely personal aspect to the discovery that one is right in the middle of history and the evolution of humanity?

Initiation must permeate and fertilize the life of civilization. An obvious and necessary task in the Christmas Conference stands at the end of paragraph 3 of the Statutes:

"These [spiritual scientific] results are, in their own way, as exact as the results of genuine natural science. When they attain general recognition in the same way as these, they will bring about comparable progress in all spheres of life, not only in the spiritual but also in the practical realm."

That means the results of spiritual science are expressed in the form of thought so that they are understandable and are not dependent upon faith. Furthermore the thought-forms are such that they enable one to reach real spiritual experience. They can fructify, transform and refashion. The evolution of the world demands that we work at the conditions under which the *werdende Mensch* can live and develop, otherwise into the abyss we shall go.

Enormous difficulties tower up before us, and we shall now examine them more carefully. We have seen that the esoteric school is the kernel of the General Anthroposophical Society and that therefore the General Anthroposophical Society is a preparatory school to spiritual experience. At the same time the General Anthroposophical Society is open to the public and will take part in the consideration of all the questions of the day: in art, science, sociology and practical affairs. How is this to be done?

Rudolf Steiner's writings contain many passages which astonish and enthuse, but they can also bring doubt. "The healthy intellect can understand anthroposophy." If we have a healthy intellect and are without preconceptions we shall be able to understand anthroposophy. It is not necessary to be clairvoyant. You can understand anthroposophy directly in your heart if you have a healthy understanding. Enthusiasm! But also doubt! There are thousands of people who have the greatest difficulty in understanding anthroposophy. Have they no healthy intellect? That is exactly what was meant in this dictum. Rudolf Steiner says that millions of people in the present day are intellectually unhealthy. The intellect has become sick. What is this sickness? If we take it in a derogatory sense we get nowhere and it does not help.

In the sixteenth, seventeenth, eighteenth and nineteenth centuries, people achieved clarity and certainty through scientific experiments with external objects. This proceeded from a healthy urge. This gave a sure foundation for self-awareness which could be built on further. Now there was a break in the twentieth century, and now another step is due without discarding the achievements of natural science, for the abilities achieved through the practice of natural science can be applied not only to external matter but can be raised and applied to the soul–spiritual with equal clarity: "Results of observation of the soul according to scientific methods."[6] The strength and clarity of this scientific method can be applied further to what is soul–spiritual. The subtitle can be extended to "Results of observation of soul *and spirit* according to scientific methods." But the following can happen through laziness. A person may feel insecure when he no longer has physical facts as a basis and so he feels fear. From this fear arise prejudices which do not stem from the natural scientific method. From this comes the irrational belief that the whole of existence is material.

Now you could say that this is a small illusion, easily overcome. But this illusion begins to solidify and gradually

32

becomes a wall, a thick wall consisting of fear, and one says to oneself: "Spirituality and spiritual beings cannot exist." A wall is created and this encloses the soul so that it is a prisoner. Such a wall is created out of weakness. It can be built on purpose by people who have the necessary knowledge and who wish to use this wall in order to manipulate other people and wield power. This process can therefore be called "occult imprisonment," and we have the widespread "occult imprisonment" of millions of people in this century. The walls prevent people making inner progress, and causes the intellect to become unhealthy. The wall has to be demolished in order to allow the intellect to regain its health. Whether this is possible depends on a person's situation, character, capability and his search for truth. How great must the search for truth be in a person in order for him to break through this wall? Can we help each other? What are the chances?

I should like to say more about the expression "occult imprisonment." As far as I know it is mentioned by Rudolf Steiner in two places. One is in his exposition of H.P. Blavatsky's biography[7] and the other time in connection with the subject I am discussing. H.P. Blavatsky had supersensory experiences, but not much thought power. She was an exceptional medium and spiritual experiences poured through her from the spiritual worlds. She had the gift of being able to impart these experiences to others in pictures, but she did not have the ability to work at her experiences with clear thinking. Then she began to reveal various things which others did not wish revealed. What did these others then do? By suggestion and hypnosis they built a wall up in H. P. Blavatsky's soul so that she could no longer recount her continued spiritual experiences. Here we have one meaning of the expression "occult imprisonment."

Rudolf Steiner mentions the other meaning in connection with walls which are built up to prevent the spread of something else which is being created with equal determination. Three days before the founding of the Anthroposophical Society of Great Britain, Rudolf Steiner said:

"Certainly the physical world is everywhere filled with spirit, but we come to wrong conclusions about the connection of the earthly world to the supramundane world unless we are able to apply real genuine spiritual research. And so as I mentioned this morning, when we accept only what comes out of natural scientific thinking this creates the occult walls of imprisonment."[8]

We should be careful how we use such a word and only give it its exact meaning. I mention that specially because the idea "occult imprisonment" has played a not very salubrious part in the history of the Anthroposophical Society where it has been used as a term of abuse. If you did not like a colleague you simply said that he was in "occult imprisonment." For decades it often happened in the Anthroposophical Society that a member who did not like another member would say about him: "You can't do anything with him, he's trapped in occult imprisonment." Then all communication would be cut off. Here we must avoid that.

Anthroposophical work is a spiritual battle. The walls of occult imprisonment must be overcome because they are to be found in every soul. They cannot be pulled down by violence or by postulating. It does not help simply to say that the spirit exists. We have to act so that the walls melt through spiritual activity in thought, so that the spiritual is present in our thinking. The individual must kindle the spiritual search in himself, otherwise the walls cannot be removed. They have to be breached by each individual. But we can help each other. We can encourage each other through human contact when we feel something in the other person, and when one discovers the corresponding searching force in oneself, and the desire to overcome preconceptions and to reach a new and direct experience.

Here we see again an important process in all anthroposophical activity: every anthroposophical activity of cognition starts *attenuated*. This is a law, and it is healthy. The student is not constrained to accept something which he then must follow blindly. Cognition starts with thoughts originating on the periphery. In the beginning these thoughts are very indeterminate. Then they have to be condensed gradually by working at them and by the continuity of this work. What happens when these world–thoughts which speak from spiritual facts, from spiritual beings, are gradually condensed? What follows is only possible when the will wakes up in thinking. If the thinking remains passive then it remains vague and disappears again immediately. If the will rises up, is freed and begins to live, then it comes from the great periphery and becomes denser and denser so that the process of cognition becomes a living reality, changing one's whole inner life.

I can now say I am not living with vague thoughts, but something is really happening in my thinking. But how does this affect my ordinary life? On the one hand my thinking is changing, but on the other my ordinary life goes on completely unchanged as if nothing had happened. That, however, is only at the beginning. As the cognitive activity begins to condense and become reality, life itself begins to change and become clearer, so that gradually both harmonize completely. Life becomes a cognitive picture. Life and cognition interpenetrate, working together. This becomes possible as the transformation takes place in our lives. Then we act from insight. If we do not act out of insight we act out of urges, social considerations, desire for power, pressures, out of all sorts of causes, but that is not free activity. Free activity arises only from insight. It comes from the spiritual which begins to work in the will, and so the will is freed from the physical urges and from the compulsions of society and begins to speak spiritually. That is the art of living. A main purpose of art is to raise and permeate with spirit what nature has created. This purpose is at the source of all the arts: painting, sculpture, architecture. In all these, substance is transformed and raised to a higher level through the spiritual activity of the artist so that the spiritual speaks directly to us in what is visible in art.

What I have described as the art of living and as art in all the various sensory areas goes beyond the sectarian. It speaks directly from heart to heart if we are conscious of it. If however we do not attempt to reach this level in the art of life and at the level of the individual arts inspired by it, but remain as we were, it does not mean that we are necessarily sectarian. We can already be completely open to the world at the first stage of the school of cognition even before we reach the next stage of artistic experience. But in practice one often becomes sectarian, especially if in one's own development one adopts thoughts without letting them permeate one artistically. Then they just remain thoughts which are retained as dogmas of faith, and that is sectarian even though the thoughts may be right. Only when they become rigid do they become dogmatic and sectarian and a chief enemy of the whole of anthroposophy, as in paragraph 4 of the Statutes where it says: "The Anthroposophical Society rejects any kind of sectarian activity." And here we must again say: We can maintain that we do not want anything to do with sectarianism and still be full to the brim with it. It is not enough just to demand that there should not be any. That is only the first awakening. We have to go on working at this problem all the time so that we overcome sectarianism. If we think that it is already overcome it pops up again through the back door and spreads out again. It is a persistent force attacking anthroposophy through the subconscious.

Laxity, lameness and passivity are qualities which open the door to sectarianism. Sectarianism can only be conquered by activity which radiates. Then the activity becomes a cultural fact with radiating power. What does it signify when eurythmy enters more and more strongly into our cultural life? It is completely unsectarian spiritual radiation made visible. But the same applies to the art of living. When this slow transformation takes place in the individual it has the power to radiate. Then new encounters occur and gradually we become aware of the tremendous tasks for humanity.

I have only alluded to this world–historical aspect. The principle of initiation descends to work in all our culture, directly, consciously so that we can know what it is all about. If we look at it in this way it concerns not only all mankind, the whole of history in general, but works concretely in those particular circumstances in which we find ourselves, as for instance in Central Europe, Great Britain, South America. The human and historical dimensions apply to all people. But in addition each individual finds himself in a narrower historical situation which can be ignored and then one lives in one's own illusions but which on the other hand can be tackled and consciously penetrated.

What has happened to Central Europe in this century? In the last century the whole spiritual development of mankind concentrated itself upon an upthrust through German Idealism. German Idealism could have led directly into Goethe-anism to spread out into a great culture for all mankind. Central Europe was the region where the principle of initiation could have best broken through to fructify the whole culture of the time. And just there where this task was taking shape a tremendous destructive force was at work. We do not need to apportion blame, and can only regard it as enormously tragic that Goetheanism was crushed and split up. The permeation of the cultural life with the principle of initiation has been maimed. We see now how we stand in the midst of the great historical situation on the one hand, and in our own local situation on the other. When we overcome in ourselves the occult im-prisonment threatening every human soul, and when we encourage other people to break down their walls, we are furthering at the same time the whole cultural task of Central Europe. That is the task of the Anthroposophical Society.

Here we have a spiritual law which we can see working in this situation. When Rome easily subjugated Greece by political, military and economic power, what happened then? I should like first to quote Rudolf Steiner:

"We should just ask ourselves whether the outer aspect is the decisive one — one nation has made another depen-dent physically and materially. We do not always see how the first nation has then become spiritually dependent on the second."[9]

Rome became dependent on the Greek culture. After conquering Greece politically, militarily and materially, Rome had to say: "You must help us, we cannot achieve anything culturally." Everything that flourished culturally in Rome came from Greece. Rome became completely depen-dent upon the Greeks when she conquered them. Thus the

Russian and American powers who have crushed and split Germany have become culturally dependent on the German spirit. They will not be able to survive without it.

Here the Anthroposophical Society has the historic task of devoting itself to the reinstatement of the *werdende Mensch* in every single human being, and also in every sphere of culture, in art, science and all practical affairs.

Now this brings us to the next domain. As long as anthroposophical activity remains on a small scale, as for example in study groups of ten to thirty people where the members meet together and work in a productive and stimulating way in a small spiritual community, you do not need to bother about money. (When I was young we had an anthroposophical study group, rented a room and in the evening we counted how many people were present and divided the rent among those present. It was paid, without funds, without financial reports, completely without problems.) But when the activity begins to grow — and it must do if we are to tackle the cultural problems — money plays a different part. If we did not allow ourselves to expand, but went back to the nineteenth century, taking the principle of initiation out of culture again, and renouncing all attempts to direct its form, we should not have to bother about money. But if we are going to go from small study groups to greater tasks we must face the difficulties and take money into consideration. Everywhere that money is present in large amounts, something takes place of which we must be very much aware.

I shall draw your attention to the situation in the summer of 1923. There was a lawsuit after the burning of the first Goetheanum. If negligence could have been proved the insurance would not have been paid. There was a police investigation and witnesses were called in a court of law.

The witnesses were able to declare that the electricity was still working as the fire burned, which proved that the fire was not caused by a short–circuit. The insurance company did not wish to pay at first, but they were compelled by the court's decision of June 15, 1923, to pay 3.2 million Swiss francs to the Building Association of the Goetheanum. That was a very large amount. Even today it is no little sum. Now many anthroposophists were very pleased they had won the case and the money was available for the second building. Even so, more donations were going to be needed, but at least it was a good start. Then Rudolf Steiner began to show the position with regard to the money given for the first Goetheanum how every franc had been given as a sacrifice with love. The people who had wished for this building for the mystery plays, for the great artistic impulse of Rudolf Steiner, had gladly given their money:

"From the Dornach Hill there shone a building in which *anthroposophical will* and anthroposophical readiness to sacrifice had been built into every cubic inch of wood and every cubic inch of stone. This moral substance had been built into the first Goetheanum.

My dear friends, now we should begin with three million francs, much of which came out of the pockets of those who not only have no interest in the Goetheanum, but who rather are interested that this Goetheanum should not exist. And when the Goetheanum will again shine from the Dornach Hill then not only will anthroposophical readiness to sacrifice be built in, but also that which is external to anthroposophy and current in the present world will be built in. Then this Goetheanum will be quite a different building from the previous one, that is from the inner spiritual aspect.

Now we are building up the Goetheanum in a tragic

direction. A tragically built Goetheanum is something different from what we began in 1913 and 1914.

For basically we were able to begin building in 1913 joyfully. but when we begin to build now — because necessity allows no other possibility than that we build — it will be almost necessary for us to begin building with tears."[10]

Now we see the enormous difference between the second building and the first: the second one had to be built, we had to do it. It is good that we could work at it, but with tears. It is a tragic building.

We must look at the whole question of money. For this leads to the threshold where the principle of initiation is to enter, no longer behind closed doors in private, but where it will enter today's culture. Therefore the power of money must be permeated and redeemed, just as the occult imprisonment in ideas must be recognized. I should like to begin tomorrow on this theme, and then come back to the Foundation Stone verse.

# 3

Yesterday I mentioned the very difficult problem concerning money and gave an example. The power of money must be illuminated in every conscious human activity. It is no good just saying money is evil. Money is a very good and neces– sary means. But it has to be permeated with consciousness. It is no good going to sleep and thinking that once there is money all will be well. It is important how we shape it, that we know where it comes from and where it is going, so that the whole force of the inner direction is not determined by money but that money is directed by people who wish to shape it. That is why Rudolf Steiner was so incisive about the insurance money. We must not misunderstand him and think we should have nothing to do with insurance, should not pay premiums or receive "bad" money. No, that is not what is meant at all. The Building Association, der Verein des Goetheanum, had taken out a policy, paid the premium and expected to receive the amount insured. If they had thought the money they received from the insurance was "bad" money they could have given it away again, but Rudolf Steiner wanted to use the money for the second Goetheanum. The second Goetheanum had to be built — it was absolutely necessary for anthroposophical activity. Rudolf Steiner emphasized sharply that those people who were only glad about the money without realizing the considerations mentioned, now formed an "opposition to anthroposophy." These are very strong words, but opposition arises if one is asleep to such money matters. At all levels of anthroposophical activity, once one has expanded beyond small groups, money has to be taken into consideration, otherwise we should have to forgo all greater activity, all impetus to culture, all participation in wider issues. It would be impossible to have our own buildings and theatres without raising considerable sums of money. Therein lies the tremendous task of realizing how money works and managing it consciously. That is the task, not just to throw money away. It is a question of overcoming a power and of transforming it. In what way is the power of money harmful if it is not understood clearly? It works into the inter-relationships of human beings.

Whenever a person works for others (and is not all work really done for other people?), when something of great consequence is done, there are deep connections of destiny, meetings of destiny, meetings of inner character and being. This applies to all human activity. Money may enter into the arrangement. If, however, the role and function of the money is not properly understood, then the activity is merely paid for and a shadow is interposed. If the work is paid for by a wage or salary without this financial relationship being properly grasped, an understanding of reincarnation and karma is prevented. A shadow interposes itself. If, on the other hand, the money question *is* clarified, then the question of reincarnation and karma is not in the least difficult to understand. Everything to do with the inter-relationships of human beings must be seen clearly and directly, and, once that is seen, the money can be sorted out and conscious arrangements made. But when the opposite happens and the money side of things is not properly understood, it inserts itself as a shadow into human relationships and you can no longer see what is happening karmically in these relationships. And that is the main danger for the present. Just think of the power money has in all international relationships: enormous sums of money going back and forth, enormous transfers of funds without a trace of direct human relationships! Then this power of money begins to work like a great anonymous mass. Of course certain people are involved who use it, but this power becomes so great that people can no longer control it. They are sitting on the back of a huge animal, so to speak, and they think that they can direct it. In reality, however, they are borne along by this great beast.

If anthroposophy is not to remain hidden — working in small, close-knit circles — but begins to work powerfully out into the world, then money must be taken into account, and indeed substantial amounts of capital, otherwise we shall not get going. Then we must look into our institutions and ask the question: is the money side of things clearly seen or not? The degree of success varies considerably. Generally a certain element always remains unilluminated, because it is very difficult to get to the bottom of this problem. Often something unclear lurks in the background. Here we have a continual task, for even if we arrive at a stage where the money is a clearly-seen means for regulating work and social relationships, and all these are clear and straightforward, one week later the whole situation can be changed. Whenever there are gaps in consciousness, an unseen power creeps in. The question has to be asked constantly and in every new situation, otherwise this power creeps in and masks what is important: human contact, human connections of destiny. We can call this sphere the "region of destiny." Here is a tremendous future task for all mankind. In this respect the General Anthroposophical

Society must be regarded as a pioneer group, because it is trying to master this region of destiny and this kind of consciousness with a force strong enough to permeate everything right down to money. Then the consciousness can work out into the world as a healing force. But if it grows slack, anthroposophy will remain a personal matter with no social and cultural impetus, it will be just a back-room affair. That is not bad in itself, but it is a much greater task for anthroposophy to step out and work into the culture and social structure of humanity.

Let us look at this field of destiny more closely. The General Anthroposophical Society is a field of destiny without set limits, growing with those who join it. Then we have to consider not only the single individual and mankind in general but also many interrelated factors. Every individual belongs to a particular nation, lives in a particular part of the world, in a particular landscape. It makes a great difference whether one works in Holland or Cornwall or Sri Lanka, whether one lives in São Paulo or Norway. In each case one has a different substance and different starting conditions for the art of living, and accordingly the results will be different.

Now we can observe the following which is very interesting. Where did anthroposophy begin? Quite clearly in the region of Germany. The whole of German culture was moving forwards and came to a critical point where a new step was due. Rudolf Steiner made this step into the sphere of general humanity where the limitations of nationality were completely overcome. The purely human received its shaping. Everything coming from nationality was a medium and a material which was worked at. The *werdende Mensch* appeared. This breakthrough took place in the German-speaking cultural region. Then the first Anthroposophical

Society began to grow, first only in the German region and then further afield.

What was the situation in 1914 just before the First World War? There was this first Anthroposophical Society, principally in Germany (with the centre at 127 Motzstrasse, Berlin) built up by Rudolf Steiner and Marie von Sivers (Marie Steiner) with many branches in Germany and then abroad, in Norway, Great Britain and so on. In Norway there were only two branches, one in Oslo and the other in Bergen. They were both affiliated to the centre in the Motzstrasse as groups of the (German) Anthroposophical Society. The groups in Great Britain were also affiliated to the centre. Then the Great War broke out. For groups in neutral Norway the affiliation created no problem, so that the groups in Oslo and Bergen remained affiliated through-out the whole of the First World War. But what about the British? Their groups were also affiliated to the centre in the Motzstrasse, Berlin, so that they were now affiliated to "the enemy." The British at once made a slight alteration: they created their own national society in Great Britain, so that they did not have their centre "with the enemy."

Then the great catastrophe, the burning of the first Goetheanum, occurred. At the same time, in the spring of 1923, the whole Anthroposophical Society was bedevilled with internal strife and unable to respond to the demands made of it. Then Rudolf Steiner took the next great step towards the Christmas Conference. During 1923, he travelled to several countries and autonomous national societies were founded in Norway, the Netherlands, Great Britain and so on, as a preparation for the Christmas Conference at the end of the year.[11] The national societies were to constitute the "International Anthroposophical Society," the "General Anthroposophical Society" (both titles were used by Rudolf Steiner in 1923, the second less often than the first). Then the programme appeared with its invitation to the "Foundation Meeting of the International Anthroposophical Society." The programme announced: "The Laying of the Foundation Stone of the International Anthroposophical Society by Dr Rudolf Steiner" on Tuesday, December 25, 1923. Wednesday, December 26, 1923: Meeting of Members. Subject: "The Future Work of the International Anthroposophical Society and the National Societies." Already on Christmas Eve before the founding took place Rudolf Steiner said:

"By hinting at moods of soul, I am indicating what it was that moved me to take on the task of being President of the Anthroposophical Society myself. This Anthroposophical Society — such things can often happen — has been called by a good many names. Thus, for example, it has been called the 'International Anthroposophical Society.' Dear friends, it is to be neither an international nor a national society. I beg you heartily never to use the expression 'international society,' but always to speak simply of a 'General Anthroposophical Society' which wants to have its centre here at the Goetheanum in Dornach."[12]

We see that the word "international" was printed on the programme, and then Rudolf Steiner dropped this term saying that it was not right. It was not a national society, it was not an international, it was the Common (General) Anthroposophical Society. What did that signify? It signified that in the General Anthroposophical Society the national element had been superseded, nothing chauvinistic remained whether German, Norwegian or French or anything else — it was simply human. "International" as a name is inadequate for two reasons. Firstly it means only *inter–national, between nations,* and that is insufficient because we are concerned with humanity as a whole and with all that is fundamentally human. Secondly, in the decade up to 1923 there was growing opposition to chauvinism and nationalism. And in 1923 "international" had a Marxist–communist stamp, and this could be quite misleading when applied to anthroposophy.

How is this common humanity related to each specific region and people? Is there a difference? Yes, indeed. The source of the work is the same but each individual has different material to work upon. Just as a choleric or a melancholic has his own material to work upon, and each his own task, so the task for each area and people is different, and while the source is the same, the fruits are different. These are all of value and one kind cannot be replaced by another.

As the individual approaches anthroposophy, he becomes at first homeless. He is torn from his natural environment, otherwise he could not understand anthroposophy. Now anthroposophy begins to work in him, but each individual is formed of a different material. He begins to transform what he has. He begins to transform his regional inheritance into new gifts with new effects and works. This General Anthroposophical Society must not be regarded as an entity with subsections, for that would be a wrong conception. Each group in a country is an independent being, and from each there flows into the whole something that is indispensable. In America there are different possibilities from those in Asia, in Norway different possibilities from those in Italy. From each part of the world come indispensable gifts so that the common human element can grow in the General Anthroposophical Society. The first impetus came from the German element but the purely national element was overcome.

When we look at this "region of destiny" we see that it is not composed of similar parts, but it is variegated, deep and strong, containing all the qualities of the whole of humanity. In this region of destiny are not only those who are still living on earth but all the friends who have died and who of course do not belong to any nation. If you had been a Frenchman before you died, you would no longer be a Frenchman in the spiritual world. You would shed your Frenchness, and it would slowly be transformed and then you would be preparing to enter your next incarnation. In this realm of destiny are the eternal individualities. But you die differently depending on whether you were an Italian, Norwegian or Frenchman. Indeed you have a different task depending on the substance from which you came. Then we have to consider all those who have not yet been born, and these comprise the majority of the souls belonging to this spiritual movement. Only a minority is incarnated in the world: the rest are in the spiritual world. Thus we have to take into consideration this whole great region of destiny and only when we bear this constantly in mind do we find the strength to penetrate clearly all earthly circumstances.

Now we come to the first mantra in the Foundation Stone verse: *Practise spirit–memory.* This brings us to the great region of destiny with the "Human–World Beings"; not only with mankind, but also with the higher hierarchies, with whom we are united, and out of whom our being stems. This world is filled with love, for all the workings of destiny are love, God's world–love, and human love in a deeper sense. The Foundation Stone is a *stone* of love. What does "foundation *stone*" mean? It is the Father–God, the primordial substance, the ground of being, but why *stone?* Is not stone too hard? Let us examine it by saying, instead of *stone,* love: *wave* of love, *water* of love, *cloud* of love, *air* of love, *fire* of love, *warmth* of love. Those are not wrong, but it would be wrong if we did not go right down to bedrock, right down to stone, where love is condensed right down to the mineral. This we have to permeate so that it is transformed: this is *the Stone of the Grail*. The Grail, a stone, is the deepest that can be won from the hardest earthly thing. It is not enough to touch it fleetingly and then ascend again. The depths must be permeated, and the Being then appears. The first mantra looks to three–dimensional space:

"Soul of Man
Thou livest in the limbs
which bear thee through the world of space
into the Spirit's ocean–being."

The world of space is permeated right down to the stone, down to the physical body, in the first mantra, where then spiritual being becomes apparent. Substance of love is the most important thing in this region of destiny. Father–God, Seraphim, Cherubim and Thrones work in the laws and events of karma.

When we regard this matter in this way we are really looking at it from a particular viewpoint. This viewpoint we can call the viewpoint of *form–conditions*. Altogether there are three main viewpoints from which we can contemplate the evolution of mankind and of the world. The other two viewpoints are the *life kingdoms of transformation* and *levels of consciousness*. The three mantras cover these three viewpoints.

What do we mean by *form–conditions*? There are three *form–conditions*. The lowest form–condition is the three–dimensional world of space. The next highest is the lower spiritual world, the astral world. The highest is the higher spiritual world, the Devachan. The first mantra takes up the point of view of the *form–conditions,* from the highest and most inward condition of being to the lowest and most external:

"And thou wilt truly *live*
in the World–Being of Man."

The next direction is quite different. Here we are concerned with becoming: "World–deeds of becoming." We are concerned with what is always happening afresh. It is the meeting of being in the human being. All is new, in every second, in every indrawn breath. Here we have:

"Thou livest in the pulsing of the heart and lung."

Here is what takes place between the blood and the air, between heart and lung. Let me pursue this further. Let us just imagine for a moment that the blood was not there, no heart or pulse either, only lung activity, inbreathing, holding the breath, then outbreathing. What would happen? The air breathed out would be exactly the same as the air breathed in. But that is not the case. Now imagine that there was only heart activity: pulse, blood, but no air from the world, no in and out breathing. The activity would die immediately. It needs to be maintained by the revitalizing encounter, but not only an *encounter* with the indrawn air, but a *unification* whereby we take in air, unite ourselves with it, and then breathe out something that has happened in the blood. Without this unification blood would immediately become dehumanized and lead to death. The breathing of the lungs would no longer be human but just something like a pump. Now we can see what happens at the interface. The most inward element in the blood makes itself open to the world and unites itself with its surroundings and there is transformation, renewal and recomposition. The important characteristic of the blood is that it never remains the same, but is always being created anew and transformed. This leads to a transformation of the whole body. The viewpoint of the first mantra is to the moulding of form and to the primordial ground of being.

The viewpoint of the second mantra is what comes into being and dies away. Here we have forming and transforming. In these activities there are two opposite tendencies. One is to go into form too much, the other is to go into form too little. A balance between these two tendencies has to be found. If the activity goes too deeply into form then it dies there and the form remains rigid and static. The activity however can enter form in such a way that in the end a transformation, a resurrection can take place. The original form is overcome and a new form is created. This is the art of life. Here too we have meeting. Active entities meet, act upon and transform each other. This happens, for instance, in our sense–perceptions. We stream out through our senses to meet and act upon our surroundings, and our surroundings stream in through our senses to meet and act upon our souls. In this meeting a union can take place in feeling. But here the two opposite tendencies can come into play to prevent a true union taking place. One tendency is for a person not to go out to effect a meeting. He withdraws into himself and cannot unite himself with the world. This tendency appears in its most extreme form in catatonic schizophrenia, in which the patient falls into a coma: he has said "no" to the world. If the oxygen–content of the breath of a normal person is compared with that of a catatonic schizophrenic we see that the latter has taken in too little oxygen and too much has been exhaled. He cannot unite himself with the world, he cannot open himself to it.

There is also an opposite illness, "a craving for oxygen" in those people who always want to experience something new. But in the healthy balance we are concerned with that fine point of contact where our own I meets the world–I; not only meets it but joins with it. That produces the qualities of our feelings. If we examine our feelings, however rich and diverse they may be, we have to admit that often we are really only spinning a web within ourselves, for we say: "How do I feel?" But if this meeting really takes place then the world begins to speak in feeling. Feeling becomes an organ of the world–speech:

"And thou wilt truly *feel*
in the working of the human soul."

In the first mantra it was "human world–being," now it is "working of the soul." That which goes on between subject and object. The soul in feeling interweaves with all existence. That is contained in the second mantra and in all exercises on the meditative path of cognition which are directed to the purification of the feelings — calmness in feelings, positiveness — so that a deepness begins to speak in feelings. Already the first chapter of the book *Knowledge of the Higher Worlds* speaks of the deepening of the inner life. When different people go through the countryside, each experiences something different. One person has a superficial shut–in kind of feeling, goes through a wonderful forest, sees nothing and only feels himself. Depending on how this plane of contact has been developed the *world* begins to speak in feeling, differently through its different qualities. A snow–covered landscape speaks quite differently from a forest of fir trees, the blue sky, a green meadow or even the sea. A richness of experience blossoms here upon the meditative path of cognition. And it is always a becoming, a forming and transforming right into the life–processes of the whole human being. This also happens in crises where one reaches a dead point and everything enters a void, a nothingness, but where a resurrection follows. Death, resurrection, a forming, a transforming. What happens here is characteristic of the life of the soul and of the second great direction. Now we are in the life–kingdoms, in the world–rhythms, in the evolutions of the course of time. The first mantra led into space as the lowest level of the form–conditions, the second to the world rhythms of time.

What is the direction of the third mantra?

"Let there be prayed from the depths
what in the heights will be granted."

It is the upward striving in the search of cognition, the strengthening of the inner forces from the weak, dead thought–shadows to a heightened activity of consciousness in which we begin to awaken. This inner strengthening of formative thinking is a principal stage on the path of meditative cognition, where the formative thinking mounts to new levels in this region. There is an awakening from below to above in this third mantra. Praying from the depths "what in the heights will be granted": World–light, world–thoughts, levels of consciousness. That is the third great viewpoint in contradistinction to life–kingdoms and form–conditions. It is the opposite of the first mantra — "Spirit–memory in depths of soul" — where the Being of the primordial ground has to be found. All three work together, with the Trinity alive within them: Father–Spirit in that which reigns in the depths; Christ–will in the surroundings re–enlivening resurrection from death, constantly reshaping life, forming and transforming feeling in the encounter:

"Thine own I
Unite
With the World–I."

And then we see the third mantra concerned with consciousness and world–light. Shall I awaken, or shall I remain asleep? The third point of view looks to the levels of consciousness: trance, sleep, dreaming, waking consciousness, or beyond to new higher levels of consciousness.

"For the World–Thoughts of the Spirit hold sway

In the Being of Worlds, craving for Light ..."

Now this follows:

"Let there be prayed from the Depths

What in the Heights will be granted.

Speaking

In the Spirit's World–Thoughts the Soul awakes."

We see these three working together and yet all three have their individual direction. The individual human being is addressed three times:

"Soul of man! Soul of man! Soul of man!"

"Thou livest ... Thou ... Thou."

After all three have finished speaking directly to the individual I in relation to the World–I, to the Primordial Ground and to the awakening in world–thoughts, in the fourth mantra the "we" sounds. "We" is not yet present in the first three mantras. There we were in the group–soul of the family, of the tribe, of the race, then we tore ourselves away from them and became exiled souls, each one for himself. Now the individual awakens to the consciousness of the common humanity of all mankind. We awaken to the plural "we":

"Warm Thou our Hearts

Enlighten Thou our Heads,

That good may become

What we from our Hearts would found

What we from our Heads would direct

In conscious

Willing."

The creation of community after passing through the

completely individual stage is a principal task of the General Anthroposophical Society; the creation of a true spiritual community in which the "we" shall be true and genuine and in which the common–I, a higher being, is present.

# 4

Today we shall start by looking at the three mantras of the Foundation Stone verse from another side and indeed from a negative side. Then we shall see three negatives which are well–known to us all, but it is very illuminating to see how different they are and how they reinforce each other.

The first Foundation Stone mantra is "Practise spirit–memory" and it goes into the "depths of soul" to the Being, to the origin. The negative in this world of space is that which is non–being, which is empty nothingness. That is the starting point for present–day civilization which sees a cosmos that is empty of being: lumps of matter whirl through vast empty spaces, and if you put all the lumps of matter together — as has been calculated by the astrophysicists — it would only make up a minute fraction of empty space. Being–less nothingness, whether stars, galaxies, suns, planets, moons or comets: all these are only different types of molecular aggregates. Matter whirls through the vast universe, and the earth is a tiny particle of dust: being–less, empty nothingness. That is the opposite of the first mantra. Now let us contrast "being–less empty nothingness" with "being." By "being" here we mean the Primordial Being, the Father–God, the ground of existence, from whom all mankind derives its being. The "being" stands in relation to the "world of space" because it extends into the world of space in which we live with our limbs.

Let us look now at the second mantra: here the motif is what is *becoming*. Things form and die, but resurrection follows death. Something new is always happening through time, in the rhythms of time that are filled with processes of becoming. In this field the soul can develop, and we can call it "the soul's field." What is the negative picture to all this? Everything disintegrates, everything is destroyed. There is nothing in the world that does not pass away after a time. Everything dies and is annihilated. Everything disappears into a black hole. Destruction and annihilation rule, and nothing is in a process of becoming. There is no going through death, resurrection and union with the World–I — but rather everything dies away and is lost.

The third mantra is "Awakening to the world–thoughts." The soul wakes to a higher level of consciousness in the world–thoughts. What do we see here as the negative? Opinion, personal opinion, personal conviction. Of course everyone has their own opinion, but that opinion is not a reality, a real thing, it is only an opinion. Personal opinions are the negative side of the third mantra.

These three negatives are very familiar to us. Who does not know the mood of the present where the whole universe is thought to be meaningless and empty; in which only particles of matter are whirling about. A plant is only a bit more complicated in the way its molecules are assembled; the animal is even more complicated and the human being more complicated still. Then everything disappears again, all is only chance coagulations in empty nothingness.

The second negative comes to expression in the mood which is no less prevalent: "Whatever is formed dies away and is destroyed!" And the third negative with regard to the search for knowledge: "You don't imagine after all that what you think has any reality. It is only your personal opinion — opinion against opinion, assertion against assertion." To this attitude belongs the tolerance to allow everything to be valid. If I have a personal opinion, I must accept the validity of others' personal opinions. And all we have is single personal opinions.

We can see how these three negatives are the common starting point for each one of us. Each one is to be found in his personal opinion, in a being–less empty space where all is dying away and vanishing in time. Now we can examine how these three negatives reinforce each other. If, when working cognitively with the third mantra, I do not succeed in emerging from my personal opinion and in attaining world objectivity, I cannot reach the Being of the world and the world becomes being–less for me. The stronger the action of the third negative, the emptier space becomes. Correspondingly if I absorb ideas from the newspapers, mass media, education, university, and so come to the conclusion that the world is meaningless and consists only of particles of matter whirling about, then I begin to think that everything which I think is only something which bubbles up in my brain and is only a notion. The idea of the meaninglessness of the world only strengthens the idea that all my thoughts are unreal notions, and the idea that my thoughts are only unreal notions only increases my feeling that the world is meaningless. And of course both these engender the conviction that no resurrection from death takes place. Everything dies away! That anything could arise again out of death is regarded as a tremendous superstition. All disappears, all is annihilated. The other way of looking at it works in an equally destructive way. If you come to the conclusion that everything is bound for destruction — it was beautiful but it is bound for destruction — that reinforces the other two directions, so that these three form a malignant trio all amplifying each other.

It is at this starting point that we all find ourselves. In this black, empty, dark space the isolation arises, for in their personal opinions individuals become more and more isolated. In this situation the individual can persist, hold out and awaken to an inner search of cognition which can overcome the three negatives. All three collapse in the face of strength and persistence in the search for truth. Then the individual begins to overcome his *opinion* and immediately it grows lighter in other directions. If we were to take no account of this and were only to work out of the third direction, we should fall back into our opinion. Progress can only be made when the three positives are working together. Just as the three negatives fortify each other in a downward direction so it is not possible to develop only one of the three positive directions. We can try that inwardly; we can say: "I will practise perceiving death and resurrection when my I meets the World–I. But on the other hand I have only a personal opinion." Then the experience vanishes. "It is not right, it is not true, it is only something I thought." You have to have all three directions integrated in the ascent, otherwise they will not work.

When we see all this we realize how strongly separated and isolated the starting–point situations are. This can be visualized by imagining a circle containing all that has being in the world, but the human being is not in the centre but right out on the circumference, each individual at a different point. Here I am on the periphery and I am not inside in the reality. Someone else does not stand here, only I stand in my body at a certain place, another person stands there, yet another over here and I cannot reach out to them — unless they all move into the true reality. If we remain on the external periphery we are hopelessly separated for all eternity — not only so separated as we are now, but the separation increases. If we study the history of the development of individuality, how the individual has developed a consciousness of his own I, and how he has come to feel himself in isolation, we can see how this hardly existed in ancient times. People then felt themselves *together,* everyone was together in a strong condition of being in a group-soul. Then each individual began to move gradually towards the periphery, a periphery which is becoming wider and wider, further and further from reality. At present we are very far out but not yet at the farthest, for the periphery will continue to expand, and the isolation will increase in the next centuries and millennia. It is the way of individualism to be at one place where one works and no one else is at the same place. The isolation of the individual will become more and more pronounced. Only when we awaken and become fully aware of it and accept it, do we see that it is the lowest point of the swing of the pendulum from group-soul community to spiritual community. We should not return to the old group–soul, nor remain in our present isolation of personal opinion, in the transient and being-less, but awaken and seek spiritual community with others. But this is not simple. If we seek "too directly" we come only to an appearance of coagulation with intensive sympathy. Then the reaction sets in, for that will not work. You cannot slip into another human being; for the more one tries and the nearer one comes, the more there will arise a hidden level of strife, for each person wants to be independent. After all we do not wish to melt into one another. The closer two people approach each other "directly" the stronger the strife in the subconscious. Then usually they bounce off each other, not always, because one may subjugate the other as there is an urge to dominate and strangely enough each soul has the potential wish to be dominated. In both cases there will not have been a meeting of being. Usually the pair split up because one wishes to be independent. Unless one wakes up to a higher level it will not work.

"The Anthroposophical Society is to be an association of people whose will it is to nurture the life of the soul, both in the individual and in human society, on the basis of a true knowledge of the spiritual world." In this first sentence of the Statutes of the Anthroposophical Society, we see in this ascent the whole impulse for the future. Individuals are not united. They begin to search. They cannot be joined together by the mere invocation: "Be clasped together, O ye millions!" That will not do. We must first ascend "on the basis of a true knowledge of the spiritual world." To rise above our own personal opinion is only possible through working at knowledge, otherwise we remain on the periphery where only a feeling of being embraced takes place, and this always dissolves again into nothingness. It is not only necessary that this ascent should take place in this or that person, but equally important is the "care of the soul-life," of what is becoming. The whole is a development which affects not only the individual by himself but also his relation to society. The three ascending directions are the conditions of anthroposophical work. The great significance of the Anthroposophical Society in the world at large and in the small branch, in the smallest groups, is this ascent from the isolation of the individual to the finding of others. Only when we first ascend do we awaken on a higher level.

Let us look more closely at this awakening by adopting the viewpoint of the second mantra with regard to consciousness. There we see ascending levels. The lowest is trance–consciousness, corresponding to the consciousness of the stone whose group–soul is in the highest Devachan. The next level is the sleeping consciousness of the plants: no dreams, no inner pictures, but already a higher level of consciousness. The next level is dream–consciousness with its inner pictures from which we awaken after sleep to our everyday consciousness. In everyday consciousness, the three negative forces are united in today's civilization. In everyday consciousness we have personal opinions: "everything is going to rack and ruin," "the world is being–less empty nothingness in a great endless space." But being together is pleasant in itself. We try to find friends and then we fall apart — strife and love, hate and love in this region — things flow together and fall apart, alternating in everyday consciousness. There anthroposophical activity is not possible. It only begins when we rise to a level above ordinary consciousness. A second awakening takes place. That begins when we succeed in holding back our personal opinion in our thinking activity and effort. The world objectivity begins to be effected in thought through the activity of the individual. It never comes by itself. Spirit–consciousness begins to awaken: that is, spiritual science. In that moment a new possibility of encounter shows itself: now you can see the other person anew, differently. Now you see him not as a soul and bodily phenomenon, but rather you see the spiritual activity in the other person, the soul–spiritual being–activity. We meet friends who are on the same path, but who have a different starting point. Then as we see how the other person is working at himself, at this struggle to ascend, we see his spirit–being's activity. We awaken to the soul–spiritual in the other person. We cannot observe the soul–spiritual unless it is active. If it is asleep it cannot be seen.

Sometimes in anthroposophical circles people speak

about "awakening to the other person." That expression is justified when it is meant as an abbreviation of the complete expression: "awakening to the soul–spiritual of the other person."

Whenever we perceive another where he or she actually stands in life, this represents a genuine encounter. Each person stands in a different field of battle to transform his life, to lead his life on through crises and difficulties. But this being works itself to the fore, it is the spirit–being in the other person. If we meet each other in this fashion, then there is no hidden struggle behind the encounter, for then we are indeed brothers and sisters and spring from a new common source. Community is formed — the meaning of the Anthroposophical Society, the General Anthroposophical Society in each little group. It always begins with the individual. Cognition cannot begin in a group, it must begin in the individual, but then we find the other person anew. In this finding anew, we receive a decisive reinforcement.

If one remains alone with one's anthroposophical work, one can go a fairly long way. Then the lone individual stands opposite the whole world. But he has no friends, he cannot see the endeavour in another person. That is one possibility: you can get quite far on your own. But when the meeting of our beings takes place, then a new level of inner strengthening is attained and continuity of experience is fostered, whereas if one is alone what one achieves is easily lost. When we work together our beings can unite even though we are separated in space at times. In this work we are creating a new and inward community.

We must now describe the laws more exactly. When we look at the first threshold of awakening, it is quite sharply delineated. Usually this applies to all normal people: you dream in the night, and when you wake up you do not dream any more. Instead you are aware of the pillows, blankets, the wall and so on. You are quite suddenly in the next level of consciousness. Of course you can remain lying in bed but you are awake and you know that you are not dreaming. But there are threshold phenomena where that is not the case. About five per cent of exceptions appear with quite normal people: for example, that you wake up in bed and know "that is the pillow, that is the wall, here is the blanket," but the dream goes on in the bedroom. It super-imposes itself, it is not imagination. Sometimes it is a bit upsetting when that happens. What is the significance of this condition? You know that you have shut the door and that there is no one in the room. Then you are awake as you think, feel the pillow, the wall and someone else is in the room. It is a hallucination, but not an unsound con-dition. There is a psychological expression for it: "hypno-pompic hallucination." This appears after sleep and intrudes into your ordinary consciousness. Usually it lasts only a few seconds, then it is gone. It can however be more protracted, and then it is very alarming, when you are lying in bed and the dream goes on in the bedroom. If it goes on into the day then you have gone mad. You are ready for the mad-house, for example, if you are walking along the street and suddenly you see a non-existent elephant coming along. That is when the dream-consciousness inserts itself into the day-consciousness and disturbs it. If only a little disturb-ance happens on the threshold that does not matter. But when it is too strong it becomes a serious matter. That only happens with a small minority of people.

On the next level there is once again an awakening. In this, "hallucinations" in a transposed sense occur also. We rise to this higher consciousness in the active life of cognition as we rise above personal opinion, meet other people, and then suddenly everyday consciousness intrudes — hallucination raised to a higher power. Now this disturbance can be very serious. The border between dream and ordinary consciousness is very thick, so that only in exceptional cases and in madness is there an intrusion. On the second level the border is a bit thinner so that here something from the ordinary consciousness can easily protrude and disturb the higher consciousness. We can see that everywhere in the General Anthroposophical Society. A person rises from ordinary consciousness to the next level of spiritual cognition and suddenly he is back in his ordinary consciousness with his personal opinions, and he injects them into the higher consciousness. Ordinary likes and dislikes which have their rightful place in ordinary life are now inserted into the higher consciousness. These are of the same nature as those disordered illusions which not only shimmer on the borders but project into ordinary consciousness, but with the great difference that when these hallucinations from the dream state are projected into ordinary consciousness, you are taken to the lunatic asylum, but when ordinary consciousness intrudes into the higher consciousness you are not taken to the lunatic asylum. We must see however how dramatic is this awakening on the second level and how if it does take place the greatest hindrances have to be overcome. If you have once woken to the soul-spiritual it is by no means certain that you will do so the next time. For this border with the second awakening to the soul-spiritual of the other person is very thin.

Is it possible to show up this hindrance more exactly by an example? When we work at spiritual cognition beyond personal opinion, it is necessary to work out strongly-formulated thoughts, otherwise we just run into a fog. Our cognition must receive a stamp. But every time we really imprint, shape and formulate a thought, the thought is inclined to die and to remain static in a dead form. This tendency is experienced by every modern person. This is not bad to start with, because we need a certain framework, but it is bad if we do not notice this tendency, for then the dead thought–shadows appear with correct anthroposophical content. When the ascent takes place a deep inner antipathy arises against what we might call "things intellectual." The thought–shadows *are* intellectual, they *are* dead shadows, but instead of overcoming that by strong thought–activity, so that we come to the spiritual realities, it often happens that people do not want to think. They want community without cognitive thinking, because otherwise it becomes "intellectual." They want to meet the other people directly in direct soul contact — but no cognitive work please. Then they sink back down, there is no longer a nurturing of "the life of the soul, both in the individual and in human society, on the basis of a true knowledge of the spiritual world." That disappears and the group is no longer an anthroposophical group.

We experience hindrances because of this obscuration when the thoughts congeal, whenever they are repeated in the same form. Instead of breaking through these to a higher activity one sinks back and does not even have clear thoughts. All that remains is an outpouring of soul, conversations without content. Then a group–soul takes charge, and this is always sectarian — just as sectarian as the thought–shadows of fixed dogmas which are merely repeated. Here we have two kinds of sectarianism.

To awaken to this next level of consciousness is a great struggle, one which is taking place in the history of mankind. As we progress we seek to reach the basis of being in the depths of the soul. On this path we encounter beings —

that is if we attain to the awakening and do not fall back into personal opinions. Now this brings me to an important point which I shall explain. There are two tendencies in the modern soul which are clearly to be distinguished: longing for being — and rejection of being. Many people, even those who take part in anthroposophical branch work, want to hear about things spiritual, about, say, spiritual laws (Metamorphosis of the plant? Wonderful! Reincarnation and Karma? Wonderful! But please, no higher beings, no angels, no archangels!). These people wish to remain in the sphere of *general* laws and ideas, without taking the next step to spiritual realities where we encounter spiritual beings. The opposite of this rejection or withdrawal from beings, this "please, no higher beings!" is present in the longing for being. Here people want a direct communication with the spiritual world — a relationship to the spiritual world, but without thinking–work. We see that there are two tendencies. But the search for being, the taking seriously of being, is essential in this field.

If we study earth–life from birth to death and then compare it with life in the spiritual world between death and a new birth, the individuality in its spiritual development shows itself in two polar opposite life–forms. During earth–life we rest in our physical and etheric bodies. How weak and thin the cognitive life of the I–consciousness is in comparison with the wonderful construction of the bones! Compare the wisdom–filled sureness in the construction of the physical body with the feeble, groping, searching activity in our own cognition. Just imagine that we should create a bone out of our own activity. We should never succeed — at best a plastic bone. There is a strong force working in the physical body and also in the etheric body. In these divine–spiritual creative acts we rest during our earth–lives. Without this we could do nothing between birth and death. On this base, deeply embedded in the forces, laws and wisdom of the physical and etheric bodies, we work more or less on the way to freedom. Then we die. The physical body is gone, the etheric body lasts another three days then off it goes into the distances. Has the poor helpless dead soul nothing to hold on to now? Will it not have to dissolve into the universe? That is not the case. From the other side comes a corresponding spiritual certainty. After the first three days when the etheric body has dissolved, the soul which has died is embedded in the hierarchies, in the higher beings, just as we on earth are embedded in the sure foundation of the physical and etheric bodies. After death we are embedded and rest in the beings of the angels, archangels, archai and the higher beings, and gradually pass through stages of development to an individual activity in the life between death and a new birth. This is very different for different people just as it is on earth. Some people are so lacking in independence, so little creative on earth that most of what they do is a reflection of the physical and etheric bodies and stems from external physical impressions. Thus there are souls who are only embedded in higher hierarchies, at least for the time being. These souls have developed no independent activity. Here follows the law: the more a person achieves on earth over and above his natural abilities by way of love and cognition, the more independent he will be after death when he is embedded in the higher hierarchies and works with them. And vice–versa: the more a person attains this independence between death and a new birth and then incarnates, the less dependent he will be on his own body. Then he can work creatively. The two things reinforce each other. So we can recognize what happens when in anthroposophical work we rise above the personal–individual and enter upon this common work in the branches and in the General Anthroposophical Society.

The angels are present whenever we awaken and are not overcome by the second kind of hallucination breaking through. What otherwise would come after death — being embedded in the higher hierarchies — begins before death to be present in this work. We find ourselves in the spiritual regions referred to by the three mantras. These kingdoms begin to appear and to work with us and are present: first the angels, they are more individual and strengthen what is individual, then the archangels who make what is going on in the individual fruitful for others so that individuals may work together. Then come the archai, the Spirits of Time who enable us to rise above sect and to integrate our work in contemporary culture. In the branches we are then working at the tasks of the present. The work is not shut away in a sect, but it is concerned with the tasks of the time. The three kingdoms of being are then present and consciously experienced.

We move on here to the point of view which Rudolf Steiner developed in the darkest hour of the Anthroposophical Society during the winter and spring of 1923, as the audience to whom he was giving his lectures had quarrelled and split into wrangling factions. At first it seemed that this ascent would not happen. Then Rudolf Steiner set out this task and compared it to the religious rites. In the religious celebration of the sacrament, something of spiritual being is brought down to earth so that it is present in the visible process of the rite, or cultus. That is not the primary task of the groups in the Anthroposophical Society, for there operates what Rudolf Steiner referred to as the reversed cultus. First the individuals through their cognitive work climb up to the next level where the angels, archangels and archai are present. Rudolf Steiner explains that succinctly:

"The anthroposophical group raises the thoughts and feelings of the assembled individuals into the supersensory."[13] This does not happen by itself. It only happens through work. Then comes the second awakening. "And when an anthroposophical content is experienced in the right frame of mind by a group of human beings, [that is the cultivation] of the soul–life in the individual and in human society on the basis of a true cognition of the spiritual world, ... whose souls wake up in the encounter with each other, the soul is lifted in reality into a spirit community. It is only a question of this awareness really being present. Where it exists and groups of this kind make their appearance in the Anthroposophical Society, there we have in this reversed cultus, as I shall call it, in this polar opposite of the cultus, a most potent community building element. If I were to speak pictorially, I would put it thus: the community of the cultus seeks to draw the angels of heaven down to the place where the cultus is being celebrated, so that they may be present in the congregation, whereas the anthroposophical community seeks to lift human souls into the supersensory realms so that they may enter the company of the angels. In both cases this is what creates community."

A true community of the future can only be formed when angels, archangels and archai are present. If it remains with human beings, either each individual is isolated in himself, or he belongs to an old group–soul in which he swims along. A true spiritual community of the future can only be formed through ascending in consciousness, through a common work in which the next highest kingdom of beings is present:

71

"A real group–spirit is similarly attracted by our common experience when we study anthroposophy together, though it is obviously not a group–soul active in the bloodstream. If we are able to sense this, we can form true communities."[14]

In the previous quotation, higher beings were mentioned in the plural: angels, archangels, archai — with three different qualities. Now Steiner speaks of "group–spirit." One being in each branch, one being in the whole General Anthroposophical Society. The Community–I is a higher being, to whom one only comes by ascending. We must simply make anthroposophy come true — come true by calling forth in our anthroposophical communities a consciousness that as people come to work together at anthroposophy, each one first awakens to the soul–spiritual in the other. Individuals awaken to each other as each in the meantime goes through something different, has come a little bit further and finds himself somewhat transformed. We perceive how the other person has worked at himself: we perceive the soul–spiritual at work. If no one has worked at himself, there is just a crowd of people, no anthroposophical group. Each one works at himself, then he ascends and perceives what is happening. The awakening is an awakening to budding and sprouting, in a process of becoming. It is the second mantra: overcoming of death, new life recurring. Then the ground of being slowly rises up into consciousness.

We might speak at length about the difficulties and obstacles. Remember that everyone has obstacles within. Every person has a powerful double, or even two or more doubles. There are all kinds of residual difficulties, obstacles, adversaries at work in each person. Also the spirit of each community has a double. These doubles are held in check when we actually ascend. But if we do not ascend, they get free play. Then the life of the group is determined by the double and not by the group–spirit. Just as each individual follows the course of life, going through crises and difficulties — and perhaps through the experience of these very crises reaches a greater awakening — it is the same with the life of a group, a community and the whole General Anthroposophical Society.

# 5

I have emphasized the importance of the work of cognition as a foundation for every activity in the anthroposophical movement and in the Anthroposophical Society. But is it absolutely essential to begin with some kind of work of cognition? Is it not possible to approach anthroposophy from quite different angles and in quite a different way? Can we not be flexible and do something else: artistic activities such as eurythmy, painting, architecture, decorating and so on? In all these activities, community can be formed and practised.

We must be quite open to such possibilities, and people who come together like this must find their own way and manner of working, according to their capabilities and circumstances. But they must ask whether what they are involved with is a social club, a kind of hobby club, or truly a cultural task of anthroposophy. This must lead to inner examination which always has three aspects. We cannot practise only the central mantra ("transformation," "the becoming" where we meet and unite) and neglect the other two. But the same applies to the work of cognition. If we imagine that it is simply a matter of cognitive work, of searching for the world–thoughts, and do not take into account the other two directions, we will not succeed, for the work of cognition would simply heap up ideas and shape them, which is an artistic activity employing the skill to formulate ideas. This construction of ideas would always be inclined to crumble. It would not be a real work of cognition, a search for truth, for in such a search one enters completely into what is happening during the search for world–ideas. With the inmost part of one's existence one enters the search and penetrates right inside the whole of world evolution. Once inside, there is always something to be done, to transform, otherwise one did not quite enter. When one does enter completely, every idea becomes an ideal. If that does not happen and the idea does not become an ideal, then it is cut off from existence and dies. Not only does it die, but it becomes harmful and even deadly. In the moment when we do enter fully, we find the second and the first mantra already there. All that is becoming, all that is being transformed, all that is being worked into, the power of the ideal towards the future, the working into the depths, all of this is already inside. Therefore the golden rule is highlighted in italics in *Knowledge of the Higher Worlds:*

*"Every idea that does not become your ideal kills a power in your soul; every idea that becomes an ideal engenders life–forces within you."*[15]

We see, wherever we begin, that we must engage the total human being. We cannot neglect or postpone anything. To attempt to transform one's life without the work of cognition has no effect and does not succeed. The whole must be engaged, the total human being, even though each one of us begins from a different point. In this task the *werdende Mensch,* the emerging human being, is present in the totality, though localized at first. We prepare to raise our ordinary lives so that we may begin to awaken to the plane where anthroposophical work begins, where encounter begins; the awakening to what is working soul–spiritually in the other person, where this reversed cultus begins.

In the sacramental rite, spiritual beings are invoked to descend and can be present in the physical–sensory form of the service. If you realize this fact, and recognize what is happening, then you will know what great power these forces have to transform our lives radically. But may we really call the reversed cultus in the anthroposophical movement a cultus? Is not that which is done too weak, pale and thin? Can it be held equal to that powerful, life-transforming element that works in the sacrament, where the spirit is brought down and is present in the sensory-physical? If we are to call it a cultus, then it must be the equal of the sacrament.

Strong and powerful forces work in the cultic–sacramental service; the same forces which were already at work in the ancient mysteries. There are four stages:

The Word, the Spirit–Being, the Logos sounds;

The Act of Sacrifice;

Transformation, Transubstantiation;

Communion, Union.

First the Primordial Word sounds. When that happens in a human soul it is a confrontation with everything that he has brought with him from the past and which no longer harmonizes with the Primordial Word, but which has fallen away and become cut off. Then every person has a certain inclination not to want to transform this part which no longer harmonizes. "I am as I am, and I do not wish to change." In that case the process of transformation ceases. The next stage is the willingness to sacrifice all that the individual has that is not truthful: the Act of Sacrifice. The third stage is not only sacrifice and dedication, for that act is the precondition for the transformation to begin. The whole human being, the whole earth can be transformed, but not if one wishes to retain what has fallen away.

Through the Act of Sacrifice the door is opened to transformation. In so far as the transformation takes place it is possible to unite oneself in one's deepest and inmost existence with this divine source, with Christ: this is communion. One only comes to communion through the preceding three stages. One cannot bypass the stage of transformation, and one comes to transformation only through the Act of Sacrifice. These are the four mighty stages that have worked through the millennia.

Let us now examine whether these qualities are in the reversed cultus. In the burgeoning work on the path of cognition there is always a first stage where we discover with astonishment something new which goes beyond our own personal opinion. If we remain stuck in our personal opinion nothing happens. But on the right path we discover new thought forms in which we feel a spiritual being is at work. Then we feel a tension between this new thing and everything we have from the past: all our opinions, pre-judices, urges, desires and wishes. We feel divided. It would be much more convenient to suppress this new thing or interpret it in a way that would allow us to keep all our old ideas and stay as we were, but we would not be treating the new thing earnestly. If however we do treat it earnestly then truth always takes precedence in the search for cognition. If something is wrong, are we able to sacrifice it for the sake of truth? As soon as we are able, we can work at our existence and gradually transform it in a process of becoming. This process always starts with thinking, feeling and willing. We can do something in thinking in order to formulate our thoughts according to the truth. We can purify our feelings in order to make them truer. We can organize our will to a truer purpose. At once the work of transformation can begin. But we must not remain obsessed with the passing thoughts, feelings and directions of will while everything else in our life is neglected. Rather we should go deeper and deeper into the whole of our life's circumstances so that they become integrated harmoniously. Soon there is no limit to where the work of transformation ends; it begins to change our whole existence. Only when we work in this direction, taking seriously everything that arises during the search for truth, do the two stages, sacrifice and transformation, begin to appear. Only then is it possible to unite with the truth–content of the matter, and be right inside it. That is communion.

It is remarkable that Rudolf Steiner discovered this truth while he was still in his early twenties. In his introduction to the publication of Goethe's scientific writings we find the famous sentence:

"The perception of the idea in reality is the true communion of the human being."[16]

When we are engaged in cognition and can perceive the reality of an idea, then the idea lights up with its own reality in its ideal and pristine state, and we are entirely united with it. We then find ourselves in communion with the deepest divinity of the universe. The predisposition to this communion lives in everybody and is integral to our working in community. Nevertheless we cannot attain to this communion before something in us has been sacrificed and transformed.

It is in this work that the seeds of the three mantras of the Foundation Stone verse are laid. This we can observe in the anthroposophical work as we see beyond the empty nothingness of the present. This work is not yet full of ripe fruits, not yet radiant with blossoms, indeed sometimes not even particularly rich in leaves. Sometimes only little sprouts with perhaps a few roots are showing. But these are the seedlings of the future which are forming and growing in a winter landscape. Imagine a great expanse of ice–cold country. The trees are without blossoms, without leaves. Snow and ice lie all around. But under the blanket of snow the seeds are slumbering for the next spring and the next summer. The plants have not yet appeared with leaves, in the radiance of blossom, in the ripeness of fruit. All is bleak. In this bleak inner starkness we become aware that the Anthroposophical movement, the Anthroposophical Society, is to be found upon a path which can be described as a winter path; a winter path through the ice–cold landscape of the present, but in which there are seeds, and these seeds are beginning to grow.

But how strongly will they be able to develop? Will they be effective in the culture of our times? After all they cannot just stay as beginnings. On the other hand it would be short–sighted to think that these seeds in the winter landscape are not worth anything until they have blossomed and produced fruit. What is important is that the seeds should be alive and show promise of future development. The possibility of development is there, but we must not underestimate the strength and power of the winter land-scape. I have already indicated the three negative pictures. The first picture is of the being–less nature of the whole universe, empty nothingness without meaning. There is the second picture: "All that comes into existence will vanish. All that is beautiful will be destroyed. Death, destruction and the void." Then there is the third picture where we remain stuck in our personal opinions, where we are unable to overcome our personal opinion and rise to what shines out from the world thoughts. These three negatives, rein-forcing each other, are not something we can simply look at and overcome. A spirit power stands behind them, working with a purpose from those depths down into which it seeks to drag mankind; it is Ahriman himself with his hosts, that spiritual being who denies the spirit in order to tear down and consume mankind. Ahriman strives to maintain a vacuum of spirit. He engenders the feeling of the void, of annihilation, and of the sense of isolation in personal opinion. This incubus lies heavily on the human soul, and opens the way for a powerful Luciferic counterstroke. We see thousands of people tiring of the cold intellectual and dead appraisal of the world, and plunging into any kind of easily acquired Luciferic bliss. We see both powers: a massive cold Ahrimanic power, strengthened by the Luciferic counterstroke of easily acquired bliss, without any work, without any inward search for truth, without courage for the laborious winter path, where the seeds have first to be nurtured before they can bear leaves, blossoms and fruit. The whole long way must be trodden with perseverance.

We have already observed that something happens in the Anthroposophical Society, as we rise to the plane of cognitive work, which may be called the reversed cultus because it contains those four fundamental mystery qualities. As we contemplate these intimate processes let us hear the words of Rudolf Steiner:

"In this way, through the work of the would-be active members, the Anthroposophical Society may become a true preparatory school for the school of initiates."[17]

It is a mystery process. If this is to be nurtured, can the door to the world be left open so that any new impulses, any kind of artistic, scientific or religious conviction, can enter and participate in this work? This becomes more of a question the more deeply we perceive this spiritual task. In the last century the doors could not have been left open, for

the culture would not allow it. Today things are quite different. Everyone is in difficulty. Either people do not notice
it and go around like sleep–walkers, or they do notice and
are afraid, for they feel that things cannot go on as they are.
It is time to wake up. Every person has within himself this
threefold Ahrimanic attacking force. We have fallen low. It
is not true to say that if you take a little thought you will
experience the divine within. To begin with we must say
that all mankind lies prostrate. But we can also say that the
door is open to the ascent, to the discovery of what is new.
This is indicated in the first sentence of *Knowledge of the
Higher Worlds:*

"In every human being there slumber faculties by means
of which he can acquire for himself a knowledge of higher
worlds."[18]

The *werdende Mensch* is sleeping beneath the surface.
Now it is time to awaken. We have on the one side,
humanity prostrate, a sacrifice and prey to the devouring
Ahrimanic and Luciferic powers, but on the other side this
seed of inner evolution in every individual. The door is
opened. Now everyone, by taking thought, can discover the
*werdende Mensch* as a reality. When this thinking activity
begins to blossom in the work of the anthroposophical
movement — on this slow, long winter path — the question
may arise: where does this new possibility come from? How
is it possible to follow this ascending path in learning when
we have been laid so low? The force is present in us and
can be perceived, but where does it come from?

The question directs us to the first mantra: "Practise
spirit–memory." Its source is the Mystery of Golgotha, the
central event in the whole evolution of the earth and of
mankind, without which the majority or all of mankind
would have been consumed in the abyss. We look back to

the turning point in time and find the source: death and resurrection. The Divinity does not live only in the far distances, creating the world. Christ is descended, has united himself completely with humanity and with the earth, through a particular human body, at a particular place, at a particular time, which thus became the turning point. He took upon himself the whole path of life and suffering that belongs to the human being, he followed it through and overcame all that it entailed. To have gone along the path of pain and through death is the deed of the Christ–being: that is the substance of love, the will to unite himself with all mankind, with the whole earth. Thus we can look back and find the source of that force active in each one of us, the force which each one of us can find directly even without knowing that it is connected with the Mystery of Golgotha. A person does not even need to know the name of Christ and yet can find this force directly in himself, but the deepened search for cognition of the spirit–memory leads him to recognize that it really comes from this source.

Here we see something completely new in our time compared with pre–Christian times. When people in pre–Christian times sought the help of the divine powers they always looked upwards to them. That is no longer sufficient, and would lead us on the wrong track. When we would seek the divine powers in ourselves, we must really look back to find something on the earth. The Mystery of Golgotha took place on earth in a certain person. It is the source and seed of the whole of the further evolution of mankind. In the first period after the Mystery of Golgotha this mystery lived as the new illuminating future force in all mankind, on the whole earth. It lived in people's feelings, but in most cases with very few exceptions people were not capable of recognizing it cognitively; it lived in the feelings, mainly in the feeling that life had to be transformed. Many, many people in the Middle Ages experienced that their lives had to be completely transformed. They could not yet discover this by an act of cognition, but were dependent upon tradition, on the continued reiteration that something had taken place. If they believed in it, then they could find the source. They found it in the feeling that their lives had to be changed. This impulse lasted for nearly two thousand years and affected millions of people. Today this impulse is no longer sufficient because the great Ahrimanic assault has implanted the threefold negative picture into everybody. However religious one is, however much one believes in Christ in one's feelings, as soon as one begins to think, one thinks astro–physically ("the sun is a ball of gas composed of molecules whirling about," and so on). We have in our heads the Ahrimanic counter–picture which has led to the building of a wall. If that were to remain, people in their feelings would also lose Christ as the source of transformation of life at a time when the Luciferic–Ahrimanic powers are so very strong and attempt to consume humanity once and for all.

Now follows the next intensification of the Mystery of Golgotha; not a repetition in the sense that a new incarnation will take place, repeating the passage through death and resurrection in one person. That happened only once in the whole of the evolution of mankind. What follows is a new stage where people become aware of the Being within them, on the level of the etheric, so that now it is possible for the human being to unite himself cognitively with this primal source. This intellectual ability to unite calmly and clearly with this Being can, however, be rejected, for this Being does not thrust himself into the human soul if the soul does not wish it. On the other hand the Ahrimanic–

Luciferic powers are searching for every chink in the consciousness whereby they can thrust themselves in despite the human will. Christ does not do that. Christ is present as a real being in the etheric, in every person, in every breath, in every movement. But every person is free to reject it.

Now the fourfold ascent becomes visible. Something new appears, and immediately there is a discrepancy between it and everything that the individual carried in himself from the past. Then defiance can arise and a person can say: "I won't, I won't have anything to do with it. I am self-sufficient as I am!" Every person has a certain amount of pride and conceit. When a person discovers what is new he faces the question: "Has truth precedence or does my own will have precedence?" It is the question of truth, the question of whether truth will be made real; the question of the existence of the whole future. On the second level, sacrifice, one is willing to give up that which has petrified and does not agree with what is new. On the next level one is not only willing to give up, but also willing to be transformed and to work on oneself. Only when the stages have been accomplished is it possible to have a true communion so that it becomes possible to say: "Not I, but Christ in me." Christ is then completely in the I of the individual: that is communion. Every person can reach this goal through the four stages of this path because the Christ-being is really present. If his being were not there, one could not reach the goal.

Note how the Foundation Stone Meditation begins in the singular. The human soul is appealed to. It speaks to itself:

"Soul of man,

Thou livest in the limbs ...

... in the pulsing of the heart and lungs ...

... in the resting head."

The soul begins to awaken and now must go deeper and deeper on the individual but threefold path of cognition: world–thought–light, transformation of life, search for being — in the middle, the powerful realization that "from death comes new life." We die in Christ, so that new life may come from death. In Christ death becomes life, becomes the seed of the *werdende Mensch*. That is all practised in the single individual. It is present in every person, and also in what happens when individuals meet, in the forming of the seed of the reversed cultus in the anthroposophical work however small and elementary it may be. Again the question arises: where does this *werdende Mensch* come from? Then our search goes back and the Mystery of Golgotha is found:

"At the turning point of time
The Spirit–light of the World
Entered the stream of Earthly Being.
Darkness of Night
Had held its sway,
Day–radiant Light
Streamed into souls of men."

Now something new comes to the fore. Two streams: Shepherds and Kings. They signify two fundamental paths of the otherwise very differentiated history of humanity, two polarities: the Abel stream and the Cain stream, both in various forms but each coming from a different direction. The main characteristic of the Kings is to be seen in their degrees of experience and wisdom achieved in the course of many incarnations in connection with the three soul–forces of thinking, feeling and will. The thinking, feeling and will of the individual human being are here developed for his cultural tasks. This development is the supreme result of thousands of years of experience. Melchior, Balthazar and

Caspar — thinking, feeling and will — the Red, the Blue and the Green King with their gifts, present a picture of the threefold work within the individual. But "every idea that does not become an ideal for you kills a force in your soul." If the Kings were only to hoard their treasure of wisdom, that would be a way of death. They do not do that. The finest of what they have achieved on their path they give as a sacrificial gift for mankind, for the source of the *werdende Mensch.*

That is the one great stream. The other stream is the pure innocent original force in every human soul which, coming from the abundance of paradise lives on in the inmost part of the heart: in the power of dedication, complete openness of reverence without knowledge, without the work of cognition, without having achieved fruits. The inmost dedication and openness of heart in the consciousness of the divine origin. The hearts of the Shepherds, who have none of the culture of the Kings, nor any of their gifts, retain the whole devotion, reverence, purity and innocence of man in paradise before the Fall. As soon as the angels appear, the Shepherds can hear them. The message sounds directly into their hearts, warming them and setting them aglow. In the Kings it is the heads which are shining. If the Kings had only heaped up treasures of rich and wise ideas, these would only have been shadows. Because the Kings sacrifice their ideas, the ideas shine forth. It is the Light of the World–Being.

These two separate streams of humanity, the Kings' stream and the Shepherds' came together to the original source: the Christ–Sun, the Sun that illuminated the heads of the Kings and warmed the hearts of the Shepherds. Since then all this has undergone a great metamorphosis. Every awakened individual, irrespective of what part of the world he comes from, has now both streams united in him in the radiance of the Christ–Sun. He can rise to the community of the "we" where also the forces of both streams are present. In the fourth verse of the Foundation Stone mantras, the "we" appears. The verse says:

"That good may become
What we from our hearts would found
What we from our heads would direct
With single purpose."

The seed is small. We are on the winter path in a winter landscape. But we are bearing the seed of the future.

When this seed begins to emerge and we see the winter landscape, we are exposed to the enormous temptation of saying: "Let us take no notice of the outer world. Let us gather together and leave the others out in the winter landscape. What we experience is too great and too beautiful for it to be impaired by this winter landscape." That is not the Michaelic path. The Michaelic path of this cultural epoch is to bring this new seed into the whole cultural life, fructifying, enlivening and renewing it. This cultural life is not to be left untended. A tremendous force of will works from the Christ–Sun not to abandon but to take part in the affairs of mankind.

Here again we see again the duality in the tasks of the Anthroposophical Society. On the one hand to activate the spiritual source really deeply and strongly, on the other to take it out through open doors into the cultural world — through the same open doors through which anyone can enter freely. This Michaelic and universal direction is a life–necessity for the whole of the Anthroposophical Society. Not the desire to withdraw but to develop one's whole inner strength and then plunge in!

If we experience difficulty in that successes are too

small, we must remember that it is a winter journey. Therefore two things are necessary. First, humility so that we do not imagine that what we are doing is bigger than it is, and become a prey to vain illusions. At the same time we must avoid the false humility of thinking: "I cannot do it." True and strong humility is to see how small our work is, but also to see the seed in the winter landscape and the whole future of mankind through centuries and millennia, and to recognize this whole life of the future in ourselves.

Second, Friedrich Nietzsche distinguished between two types or qualities of will. He mentions "short will." This is quite normal and necessary: for example to take a book from here and put it there; will, execution, success or failure. Then Nietzsche says: "There is also a long will." This has not such short and immediate aims, where I only carry out this or that minor action. In the anthroposophical movement we need the long will of perseverance, whatever happens, whatever defeats, whatever opposition may come: the perseverance of the seed in the winter landscape.

# Notes

1. *Awakening to Community* (Lecture 1). Anthroposophic Press, New York 1974. p.18.
2. Published in *The Foundation Stone,* Steiner Press, London, 1979.
3. Translated from Marie Steiner, *Rudolf Steiner und die Zivilisationsaufgaben der Anthroposophie. Ein Rückblick auf das Jahr 1923.* Dornach 1943, p.114.
4. *Anthroposophical Leading Thoughts.* Steiner Press, London, 1973, p.40.
5. *The Anthroposophic Movement* (Lecture of June 11, 1923). H. Collison, London 1933.
6. Rudolf Steiner, *The Philosophy of Freedom.* Steiner Press, London 1979.
7. Rudolf Steiner, *The Occult Movement in the Nineteenth Century* (Lecture of October 11, 1915). Steiner Press, London 1973.
8. From: *Rudolf Steiner und die Zivilisations...* pp.151, 153. See note 3.
9. From: *Rudolf Steiner und die Zivilisations...* p.154. See note 3.
10. Rudolf Steiner: *Aufbaugedanken und Gesinnungsbildung.* Dornach 1942, p.13ff.
11. From: *Rudolf Steiner und die Zivilisationsaufgaben.* See note 3.
12. *The Christmas Conference.* Anthroposophic Press, New York, 1990, p.51.
13. *Awakening to Community* (Lecture 9). See note 1.
14. *Awakening to Community* (Lecture 6), p.99. See note 1.
15. Rudolf Steiner, *Knowledge of the Higher Worlds.* Steiner Press, London 1969, p.31.
16. Rudolf Steiner, *Goethes Naturwissenschaftlichen Schriften.* (GA 1), Chapter 6, Goethes Erkenntnis-Art.
17. *Anthroposophical Leading Thoughts,* p.40. See note 4.
18. *Knowledge of the Higher Worlds,* p.19. See note 15.

# The Foundation Stone

Translation of the printed version by Michael Wilson (and George Adams where the written differs from the spoken version)

Soul of Man!
Thou livest in the Limbs
Which bear thee through the world of Space
Into the Spirit's ocean-being.
Practise *Spirit-Recalling*
In depths of soul.
Where in the wielding Will
Of World-creating
Thine own I
Comes to being
Within God's I.
And thou wilt truly *live*
In the World-Being of Man.

For the Father-Spirit of the Heights holds sway
In depths of Worlds begetting being:
Seraphim, Cherubim, Thrones!
Let there ring out from the Heights
What in the Depths is echoed
Speaking:
*Ex Deo nascimur.*
The Spirits of the Elements hear it
In the East, West, North, South,
May human beings hear it.

Soul of Man!
Thou livest in the beat of Heart and Lung
Which leads thee through the rhythm of Time
Into the realm of thine own soul's feeling.
Practise *Spirit–Awareness*
In balance of the soul,
Where the surging deeds
Of the World's Becoming
Thine own I
Unite
With the World–I.
And thou wilt truly *feel*
In the Soul–Weaving of Man.

For the Christ–Will in the encircling Round holds sway
In the Rhythms of Worlds, bestowing Grace on the Soul:
Kyriotetes, Dynamis, Exusiai!
Let there be fired from the East
What in the West is formed
Speaking:
*In Christo morimur.*

The Spirits of the Elements hear it
In the East, West, North, South,
May human beings hear it.

Soul of Man!
Thou livest in the resting Head
Which from the grounds of Eternity
Opens to thee the World–Thoughts.
Practise *Spirit–Beholding*
In stillness of thought,
Where the eternal aims of Gods
World–Being's Light
On thine own I
Bestow
For thy free Willing
And thou wilt truly *think*
In the Spirit–Foundations of Man.

For the World–Thoughts of the Spirit hold sway
In the Being of Worlds, craving for Light:
Archai, Archangeloi, Angeloi!
Let there be prayed from the Depths
What in the Heights will be granted
Speaking:
*Per Spiritum Sanctum reviviscimus.*

The Spirits of the Elements hear it
In the East, West, North, South,
May human beings hear it.

At the turning of the time
The Spirit–Light of the World
Entered the stream of Earthly Being.
Darkness of Night
Had held its sway,
Day–radiant Light
Streamed into souls of men.
Light that gives warmth
To simple Shepherds' Hearts
Light that enlightens
The wise Heads of Kings.

Light Divine
Christ–Sun
Warm Thou our Hearts
Enlighten Thou our Heads,
That good may become
What we from our Hearts would found
What we from our Heads would direct
In conscious
Willing.

# Der Grundstein

The printed version


    Menschenseele!
Du lebest in den Gliedern,
Die dich durch die Raumeswelt
In das Geistesmeereswesen tragen:
Übe *Geist–Erinnern*
In Seelentiefen,
Wo in waltendem
Weltenschöpfer–Sein
Das eigne Ich
Im Gottes–Ich
Erweset;
Und du wirst wahrhaft *leben*
Im Menschen–Welten–Wesen.


Denn es waltet der Vater-Geist der Höhen
In den Weltentiefen Sein-erzeugend:
Ihr Kräfte-Geister
Lasset aus den Höhen erklingen,
Was in den Tiefen das Echo findet;
Dieses spricht:
Aus dem Göttlichen weset die Menschheit.
Das hören die Geister in Ost, West, Nord, Süd:
Menschen mögen es hören.

Menschenseele!
Du lebest in dem Herzens-Lungen-Schlage,
Der dich durch den Zeitenrhythmus
Ins eigne Seelenwesensfühlen leitet:
Übe *Geist-Besinnen*
Im Seelengleichgewichte,
Wo die wogenden
Welten-Werde-Taten
Das eigne Ich
Im Welten-Ich
Vereinen;
Und du wirst wahrhaft *fühlen*
Im Menschen-Seelen-Wirken.

Denn es waltet der Christus-Wille im Umkreis
In den Weltenrhythmen Seelen-begnadend:
Ihr Lichtes-Geister
Lasset vom Osten befeuern,
Was durch den Westen sich formet;
Dieses spricht:
In dem Christus wird Leben der Tod.
Das hören die Geister in Ost, West, Nord, Süd:
Menschen mögen es hören.

Menschenseele!
Du lebest im ruhenden Haupte,
Das dir aus Ewigkeitsgründen
Die Weltgedanken erschliesset:
Übe *Geist-Erschauen*
In Gedanken-Ruhe,
Wo die ew'gen Götterziele
Welten-Wesens-Licht
Dem eignen Ich
Zu freiem Wollen
Schenken;
Und du wirst wahrhaft *denken*
Im Menschen-Geistes-Gründen.

Denn es waltet des Geistes Weltgedanken
Im Weltenwesen Licht-erflehend:
Ihr Seelen-Geister
Lasset aus den Tiefen erbitten,
Was in den Höhen erhöret wird;
Dieses spricht:
In des Geistes Weltgedanken erwachet die Seele.
Das hören die Geister in Ost, West, Nord, Süd:
Menschen mögen es hören.


In der Zeiten Wende
Trat das Welten-Geistes-Licht
In den irdischen Wesensstrom;
Nacht-dunkel
Hatte ausgewaltet;
Taghelles Licht
Erstrahlte in Menschenseelen;
Licht,
Das erwärmet
Die armen Hirtenherzen;
Licht,
Das erleuchtet
Die weisen Königshäupter.


Göttliches Licht,
Christus-Sonne
Erwärme
Unsere Herzen
Erleuchte
Unsere Häupter,
Daß gut werde,
Was wir
Aus Herzen gründen,
Was wir
Aus Häuptern
Zielvoll führen wollen.